WE ARE ALL ENTERING THE NEW WORLD OF COMPUTERS.
BUT WE HAVE TO SPEAK THE LANGUAGE.

THE ILLUSTRATED COMPUTER DICTIONARY

In the new computer age, if you think a *menu* is used for ordering food, you're bound to go hungry. More and more, computer technology is entering our everyday lives, our homes, our schools, our offices and our language. Even if you are not prepared to purchase your own computer, you'll be surprised at how often you will refer to this invaluable guide—if only to communicate with your kids!

From analog to ZILOG, from Atari™ to Wang™, *The Illustrated Computer Dictionary* will make living in the computer age a thousand times easier.

1000 WORDS AND DEFINITIONS.
1000 GOOD REASONS TO BUY THIS BOOK.

Bantam Books of Related Interest
Ask your bookseller for the books you have missed

THE FRIENDLY COMPUTER BOOK: A
   SIMPLE GUIDE FOR ADULTS by Gene Brown
MASTERING YOUR TIMEX SINCLAIR 1000™
   PERSONAL COMPUTER by Tim Hartnell and
   Dilwyn Jones

THE ILLUSTRATED COMPUTER DICTIONARY

The Editors of
Consumer Guide®

BANTAM-BOOKS
TORONTO · NEW YORK · LONDON · SYDNEY

THE ILLUSTRATED COMPUTER DICTIONARY

A Bantam Book / October 1983

*Text and illustrations designed by Dona Z. Meilach
and Allen E. Meilach.*

*Illustrated by: Richard Flory
Technical Consultant: Michael D. Uretz*

ISBN 0-553-23871-X

Published simultaneously in the United States and Canada

---

*Bantam Books are published by Bantam Books, Inc. Its
trademark, consisting of the words "Bantam Books" and
the portrayal of a rooster, is Registered in U.S. Patent and
Trademark Office and in other countries. Marca Registrada.
Bantam Books, Inc., 666 Fifth Avenue, New York, New York
10103.*

PRINTED IN THE UNITED STATES OF AMERICA

O   0 9 8 7 6 5 4 3 2 1

ACRONYM SYMBOLS

A The letters in the acronym are pronounced
  individually. For example, in CRT (cathode ray
  tube), each letter is pronounced.

B The letters in the acronym are read as one word.
  For example, DOS (disk operating system) is
  pronounced as though it rhymed with "boss."

C The first letter (or each letter within the first
  group of letters) is pronounced separately, but
  the remaining letters are pronounced as one word.
  For example, in VTOC (Volume Table of
  Contents), the first letter is pronounced separately
  as "vee" and the following letters as in the word
  "talk."

INTRODUCTION

As computer technology infiltrates our society and more people become intrigued, involved, and confused by new terms and new meanings for old terms, definitions have to be constantly updated and refined.

The *Illustrated Computer Dictionary* contains more than 1,000 of the most frequently used words and terms involved in the purchase and use of a personal computer. These terms have been carefully selected as those most likely to confront the novice when dealing with this emerging new language within a language. In addition to terms of value to all users because of their frequency of use, emphasis is on the latest in graphics, telecommunications, and education. Considerable attention also has been given to areas of specialized interest such as word processing, business applications, and unusual equipment or program capabilities.

As an aid in handling potential problems likely to arise during use of the computer, we have included terms that relate to potential malfunctions and to error-handling routines. Whenever possible, context has been noted so that the user will understand when and why a term is likely to be used. Examples frequently have been included.

Whether you are beginning to think about owning a computer for business, home, or school or if you already own one but are unsure of what it can do for you, this sensible, comprehensible, valuable reference will help you interpret the advertisements, magazines, and manuals to guide you through the computer revolution. We are confident that the terms selected will help the user rapidly move from beginner to intermediate and advanced degrees of computer literacy.

HOW TO USE THIS DICTIONARY

We have attempted to keep this reference handy, logical, and easy to use. Terms of more than one word have been alphabetized as though they were a single word and are in alphabetical order regardless of hyphens and spaces. Generally, a multiple-word entry will be found under the first word and not cross-referenced under the second word unless warranted by popular usage; for example, central processor will be listed under *central* and not under *processor*. However, the term *local area network* will be listed under *local,* and under *LAN* with reference to *network, local area,* where the definition will be found.

All acronyms (e.g., *CRT* for cathode ray tube) have been alphabetized as though they were full words so that they will be easy to find. They are then referenced to their compound term, if necessary. The definition usually will appear with the full word unless the acronym is the more widely recognized and used of the two. Pronunciation of acronyms is divided into three categories: letters pronounced individually; letters read as one word; first letter pronounced separately and the remaining letters as one word. Symbols are used to indicate the category for each acronym.

Terms that begin with numerals have been listed as though the numeral were spelled out (for example, *8-bit* is placed as though it were spelled out as *eight*). Specific microprocessors with numerals that are names will be found under *microprocessors* with the number following, such as 8080, 8086, 68000, etc.

A

B abend <u>ab</u>normal <u>end</u>ing (acronym). Early termination of a computer program due to an error.

abort To stop or cancel a procedure or selection in progress.

absolute address The actual, physical location in storage of a piece of data that the control unit can address directly.

absolute maximum rating A machine's maximum limits with respect to the environment in which it can function, as indicated in its specifications, and which should not be exceeded.

access The ability to obtain data from and/or place it into memory.

access time The time it takes for information to become available once it has been called for via a control signal.

accumulator A location within the arithmetic and logical unit that temporarily stores the results of arithmetic or logical operations. A computer often has more than one accumulator.

accuracy-control characters Characters that indicate whether data are incorrect, may be disregarded, or are not valid for representation on the device being used.

B ACK <u>ACK</u>nowledge (acronym).

acknowledge (ACK). A control signal verifying that a block of transmitted information has been accepted by the receiver.

acoustic coupler A device, usually used with a modem, that allows a telephone to transmit digital data over an ordinary telephone line. The coupler permits the telephone headset to be placed in a cradle, linking the computer at one end of the phone line and a peripheral device at the other. See modem.

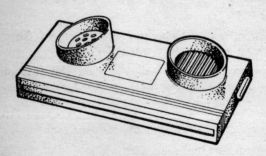

modern acoustic coupler

acronym A word formed from the initial letter or letters of each of the successive parts (or major parts) of a compound term. The result is almost always expressed in capital letters. The letters may be pronounced individually or read as a word. Example: CPU = <u>C</u>entral <u>P</u>rocessing <u>U</u>nit, with each letter pronounced individually.

A A/D <u>A</u>nalog to <u>D</u>igital (acronym).

Ada A high-level language developed by the U.S. Department of Defense, designed to establish a common language for all of its military computer projects. Ada compilers and their use are becoming more widespread. The most unique and revolutionary aspect of the language is its ability to recognize Englishlike words for easy use. Its organization relies on building-block modules and encourages combinations of smaller units so that the user can form hierarchies and nested structures.

Add The process of increasing or decreasing (if adding a negative number) a number using an arithmetic operation involving a second number.

add-on The ability to increase memory capacity, modify architecture, or otherwise upgrade performance or capability by attaching circuitry or components.

address An identification, represented by a name, label, or number for a register or location in storage.

A ADP <u>A</u>utomated <u>D</u>ata <u>P</u>rocessing (acronym). Also electronic data processing (**EDP**).

Adventure A popular computer game that originated on main-frame computers, but has been adapted to microcomputers. The player overcomes underground dangers while seeking treasure. Also a genre of a specific type of computer game.

A AI <u>A</u>rtificial <u>In</u>telligence (acronym).

alarm system A system that sends an alarm indicator for display when a critical deviation from normal input/output conditions occurs.

B ALGOL <u>ALGO</u>rithmic <u>L</u>anguage (acronym).

algorithm A finite step-by-step procedure made up of mathematical and/or logical operations designed to solve a problem.

algorithmic The procedure of obtaining an end result through a planned number of component steps.

alignment Adjustment of tolerances within the mechanism of a device so that it will operate smoothly and correctly.

all-in-one-microcomputer A computer system consisting of major systems components—a central processing unit, memory, input/output interfaces, circuitry, disk drives, cathode ray tube screen, and keyboard—all within a single housing. Contrast with individual units (see module) combined to become a total system.

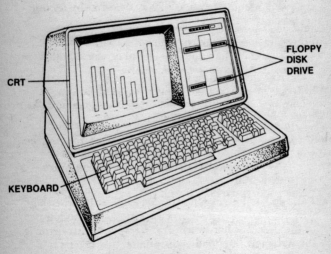

all-in-one microcomputer

alphanumeric Consisting of letters, punctuation marks, numbers, and special characters.

Altos A manufacturer and distributor of personal computers and business systems.

A **ALU** Arithmetic and Logical Unit (acronym).

American Standard Code for Information Interchange (acronym). See ASCII.

A **A/N** Alphanumeric (acronym).

analog A representation of numerical quantities using continuously changing physical quantities as a reference. For example, sound is a wave form whose transition between loud and soft is a range of continuous changes; each level merges with and blends into the next.

analog to digital (A/D). Changing or converting analog (continuous) representations of some physical quantity such as music into a form suitable for digital (separate, distinct) computer processing; i.e., into a binary system that is signified by an on or off electrical signal. See binary system.

AND A Boolean operative (or connective) whose definition is that the output is 1 only when both inputs are 1. See Boolean Algebra.

B ANSI <u>A</u>merican <u>N</u>ational <u>S</u>tandards <u>I</u>nstitute (acronym). A committee that establishes standards for data processing and computers.

anthropomorphic image A figure of speech to describe computers, computer procedures, and objects controlled by computers, as though the computer were a person.

antialiasing On a graphics display, any technique that will diminish the error that appears as a function of the graphics hardware. An example of this error is the common "stepped" appearance that occurs when displaying a "straight" line on a raster display.

ALIASED
IMAGE

ANTI-ALIASED
IMAGE

anti-aliased image

B APDOS APple Dos Operating System (acronym).

A APL A Programming Language (acronym). A
high-level programming language that uses
specially developed arithmetic operations. It is
considered a powerful language for algorithmic
interactive programming and mathematical
procedures, particularly those involving arrays.

Apple™ A manufacturer of computer systems and
software.

applications software Programs designed to handle
specific types of information and achieve useful
results or answer problems; e.g., cost analysis,
real estate management, word processing, etc.
These are purchased or written by the user and
stored on magnetic disks, tapes, or other storage
media. Documentation in the form of booklets or
manuals is often supplied to instruct the user
about the operations involved. Compare with
systems software.

architecture The arrangement, design, and
interconnection of components within the system.
Also refers to the internal design of the
microprocessor.

argument A variable within a function. The value of
the function is dependent on that of the variable;
as each new argument value is substituted, the
value of the function can be determined. The
value of the argument can be passed from the main
routine to a subroutine or function and then back
again. It is possible to have more than one argument
for a function or subroutine.

arithmetic and logical unit (ALU). An essential
hardware component of a central processor that carries
out arithmetic (addition, subtraction, etc.) and
logical (AND, OR, NOR, etc.) operations on data.

arithmetic expression A meaningful combination of
data numbers, names, and arithmetic operations.

arithmetic shift Movement of digits to left or right in computer memory, resulting in a multiplication or division of the number by 2.

B ARPANET <u>A</u>dvanced <u>R</u>esearch <u>P</u>rojects <u>A</u>gency <u>NET</u>work (acronym). A project developed by the U.S. Department of Defense in 1968 to implement a nationwide computer network. Its goals are to permit computer resource sharing, to develop highly reliable and economic digital communications, and to enable access to unique and powerful facilities that become economically feasible when widely shared.

array A set of data, usually ordered in such a way that each element of the set can be uniquely identified by the name of the set and of the position of the element within the set. An array can be more than one dimensional; e.g. a two-dimensional array would have both horizontal and vertical directions.

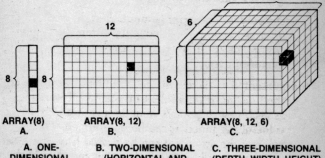

array

artificial intelligence (AI). (1) The study of computer techniques that mimic certain functions typically associated with human intelligence. (2) The study of methods for developing machines capable of improving their own operations as a result of repeated experience with a given set of problems.

B ASCII <u>A</u>merican <u>S</u>tandard <u>C</u>ode for <u>I</u>nformation
<u>I</u>nterchange (acronym). Pronounced "askee," this
standard for data transmission assigns individual
seven-bit codes to represent each of a specific set
of 128 numerals, letters, and special controls.

ASCII keyboard A keyboard comprised of most or
all characters of the ASCII character set. Most
microcomputer keyboards utilize the ASCII character
set. Each key, as it is depressed by the user,
causes the appropriate ASCII code to be sent
to a memory location in the computer. See ASCII.

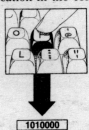

ASCII keyboard

aspect ratio In computer graphics, the ratio of the
horizontal to vertical dimensions of a frame or
image. The ability to maintain or control this ratio is
important in the transfer and reproduction of an
image on various types of display or in printed
material.

**VERTICAL
GREATER THAN
HORIZONTAL**   **NORMAL**   **HORIZONTAL
GREATER THAN
VERTICAL**

aspect ratio

assembler A computer program that translates assembly language (symbolic source code) instructions as input into machine-language instructions (binary object code) so that it can then be executed by the hardware on a step-by-step basis.

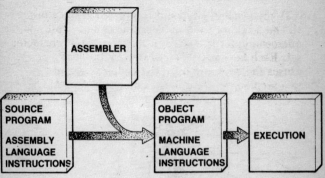

assembler

assembly language A programming language unique to each computer on which it is used and which is more advanced than machine language but less advanced than high-level language in terms of ease of use. An assembly language consists of names that serve as symbolic codes to represent binary machine instructions and addresses on a one-to-one correspondence. The user can create his own codes for addresses, and the resulting language is easier to remember and use than machine language. This machine-dependent, low-level language requires an assembler in order to translate the assembly language into machine language for execution.

```
- - - - - - - - - -
MVI    A,58H
IN     03
ANI    01
```

assembly language

associative memory A high-speed memory search based on data content rather than addresses.

associative storage Identification of storage by its content, not by its location or its name. Same as content-addressed storage.

asynchronous transmission A means of transmitting data in which a timing synchronization between the sending and receiving devices is not needed in order to decode the characters. Instead, each character is surrounded by one or more start and stop bits in order to designate the beginning and ending points of the information.

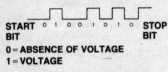

START 0 1 0 0 1 0 1 0 **STOP**
BIT   **BIT**
0 = ABSENCE OF VOLTAGE
1 = VOLTAGE

asynchronous transmission

Atari™ A manufacturer of personal computer systems and electronic games.

attribute (1) A descriptive characteristic of the data, such as a category (example, freight number), its location, or length of word size. (2) Property of a computer device.

audio-cassette recording A common serial access mass storage method using a standard home cassette tape player in combination with thin magnetic recording tapes stored in a plastic housing (cassette). To enable these standard home cassette players and tapes to be utilized with computers, tonal frequencies are used to represent 0's and 1's instead of employing direct digital recording. See digital recording; redundant recording.

audit trail A method of following and recording data from the input stage through any transitions to the output stage. An audit trail can be used to trace an input or output error to its source, verify steps that have taken place during a certain process, or recover data lost during a hardware failure.

auto-answer The ability of a modem to answer automatically incoming telephone calls.

auxiliary data Data that are related to other data but are not part of it; e.g. back-up data.

auxiliary storage (1) Same as mass storage. (2) One of several alternative types of storage media that is slower but less expensive.

availability A rating that indicates the amount of time that data processing equipment operates without error; expressed in %.

axes In a two-dimensional coordinate system, lines used as references for horizontal (x) and vertical (y) measurement in graphic representation. See coordinate system.

B

background noise Disturbance that interferes with operation of the microprocessor, usually extraneous information that must be taken out when the data are used. Often introduced in the form of electrical current.

backplane See mother board.

back up Duplication of a program or file onto a separate storage medium so that a copy will be preserved against possible loss or damage to the original.

back-up The duplicate copy on a separate storage medium, serving as a guarantee in the event of damage to or loss of the original.

bar code An identification code appearing on retail product packaging and, less often, as the medium for programs and data storage. The code consists of light and dark lines used to represent data. The codes are scanned and decoded.

bar code

bar-code reader A styluslike device used to read optical bar codes printed on product labels of retail items. Also optical wand.

bar-code reader

base The number of unique, representative symbols used in a number system, beginning with zero. For example, base 2 has numbers 0 and 1. Also radix.

baseband transmission A means of using low-frequency transmission of signals across coaxial cables for short-distance, local-area network (LAN) transmission. Contrast with broadband transmission; see network, local-area.

B BASIC <u>B</u>eginner's <u>A</u>ll-purpose <u>S</u>ymbolic <u>I</u>nstruction <u>C</u>ode (acronym). A high-level language developed at Dartmouth College that is among the most popular languages used in programming for microcomputers. It is often considered easier to learn than other programming languages because it permits more interaction between the user and computer.

```
10 REM PRINT NOS. FROM 1 TO 100
20 FOR A 1 TO 100
30 PRINT A
40 NEXT A
50 END
```

BASIC program

basic input/output system (BIOS). A part of the CP/M operating system consisting of drivers and other software that manage the peripheral devices. It usually needs to be modified each time a peripheral device is changed.

batch processing A method by which many input items are accumulated over time and are grouped for processing during one machine run. It is usually associated with punch cards. Interactive communication between user and program is not possible.

baud rate A measure for the speed at which transmission is sent from one computer to a peripheral device or from one device to another. In most systems, it is the number of bits of information transmitted per second (bps). Common baud rates are 110, 300, 1,200, and 9,600. As a general guide, division by 10 usually gives an approximation of the number of English words transmitted per minute.

A BCD <u>B</u>inary-<u>C</u>oded <u>D</u>ecimal (acronym).

benchmark A measured point of reference from which comparisons of any kind may be made; often used in evaluating hardware and software or in comparing computers against one another.

bidirectional printing A type of printer head motion that allows the head to alternate a left-to-right motion with a right-to-left motion on each successive line of print. This is a faster technique than some printers, which, like conventional typewriters, always return to the left margin to begin a new line.

binary-coded decimal representation (BCD). A method of using groups of four binary digits to code separately each individual digit of a decimal number. These binary digits are actually ASCII code for the decimal number, but since the three digits at the extreme left of the seven-bit ASCII code are the same for representations of 0_{10} through 9_{10}, these three digits are dropped off in use, which leaves a four-digit code.

UNUSED DIGITS	BINARY REPRES.	BCD
011	0000	0
011	0001	1
011	0010	2
011	0011	3
011	0100	4
011	0101	5
011	0110	6
011	0111	7
011	1000	8
011	1001	9

3   5

0	0	1	1	0	1	0	1

ONE BYTE

binary-coded decimals

binary system A system of numbers that has two as its base and uses only combinations of the digits zero

(0) and one (1). This mathematical system is based on the addition of progressive powers of two. It works conveniently in computers because its two states, zero and one, can be signified by the two states in computer circuitry—on and off—indicated by the presence or absence of voltage.

B BIOS Basic Input Output System (acronym).

bistable Refers to a circuit that can assume one of two states; application of an energy pulse will cause a reversal, so that if the current state is 1, it becomes 0, and vice versa. Same as flip-flop.

B bit binary digit (acronym). (1) The most basic element of a binary number, consisting either of a 1 or a 0. Grouped bits are used as codes to represent different kinds of information to the computer. Common group sizes are 4 and 8 bits, called words. See word size; byte; nibble. (2) The most elementary data representation in the computer; each bit takes up one unit of storage space. Usually, the presence of voltage indicates a 1, while the absence of voltage represents a 0.

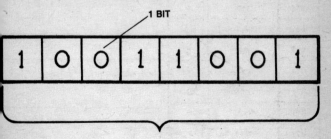

1 BIT

| 1 | 0 | 0 | 1 | 1 | 0 | 0 | 1 |

ONE 8-BIT WORD

bit

block A generic term for any kind of grouped data (bits, bytes, words, records) handled as a single unit. It is often associated with a contiguous group of records on a disk and is accessed as a unit. See record.

block move Moving a block of data or text as a single unit.

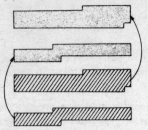

block move

block sort A sorting method that first sorts the data into smaller groups for further sorting.

block transfer Moving an entire block of data either from one memory location to another or between a memory location and an external device.

board See printed circuit board; card.

Boolean Algebra An algebraic system that relates logical functions instead of numbers. Boolean operatives such as "AND," "OR," and "NOR" are used to compare one expression to another. This symbolic representation of logical relationships, using Boolean operatives, is called algebra because it involves various rules used in algebra. In terms of computer technology, logical operations using Boolean Algebra result in conditions (or decisions) that serve as input into branching operations in

LOGICAL OPERATOR	SCHEMATIC SYMBOL	SPOKEN LOGICAL STATEMENT	BOOLEAN EQUATION	TRUTH TABLE		
				A	**B**	**X**
AND	A B —X	X IS 1 IF A & B ARE 1 OTHERWISE X IS 0	$X = A$ AND B $X = AB$	0 1 0 1	0 0 1 1	0 0 0 1
				A	**B**	**Y**
OR	C D —Y	Y IS 1 IF C OR D IS 1 OTHERWISE Y IS 0	$Y = C$ OR D	0 1 0 1	0 0 1 1	0 1 1 1

Boolean Algebra

computer programs. The output indicates the next step to be taken.

bootstrapping The process of initializing the computer for use by automatically clearing memory and loading the first few instructions. This is all the computer needs in order to get itself started. The term is based on the term "to pull oneself up by the bootstraps." Also called booting.

branch An instruction of a program that will, if certain conditions are satisfied, cause transfer from the current sequence of instructions to a different sequence. If the condition is not satisfied, the transfer will be to the next instruction in sequence. See conditional branch; unconditional branch.

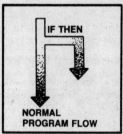

branch

breadboard An experimental model of a circuit, usually roughly conceived, that fastens temporarily to a board and can be used as a prototype in

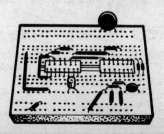

breadboard

planning, design, and feasibility studies. Blank circuit boards are available for experimental circuit-design purposes. See printed circuit board.

break An interruption of a transmission.

break key A keyboard key that tells the computer to stop what it is doing and wait for further instructions.

breakpoint Typically associated with on-line debugging. A programmer, while testing the program, will stop the execution at various "breakpoints" in order to monitor progress. In addition to examining variables at breakpoints, the programmer also can temporarily change the variables in order to test different conditions within the program.

briefcase computer A category of computers characterized by their briefcaselike size and shape, made possible in part by the use of a flat-panel liquid crystal display (LCD) rather than a cathode ray tube (CRT) display. Briefcase computers usually are larger than hand-held computers but are smaller than "portable" computers that have a CRT screen.

briefcase computer

broadband transmission A high-frequency mode of transmission often used with local-area networks, which may use coaxial cable and permit longer transmission distance than is possible with baseband transmission. See network, local-area.

broadcast Simultaneous transmission of information to a number of terminals.

bubble sort A program that can be written by the user, or purchased, to sort many types of data. The sorting is accomplished by exchanges of pairs of numbers. It is often considered relatively fast and easy to program, but it is slow in execution.

buffer (1) Any device that stores information temporarily during data transfer, internally or externally, to compensate for differences in rates of data flow. For example, without a buffer in a CRT terminal, characters transferred to the terminal from the CPU that would not immediately fit would be lost. (2) An assigned part of memory used as a holding area or a feature of a peripheral device such as a printer.

bug A mistake, malfunction, or defect in any part of the computer, the program, or the system.

bulletin board See electronic bulletin board.

burn-in Refers to operation of a new device off the assembly line for a specified initial time period, often at the limits of operating temperature, in order to pinpoint component failures due to defective manufacture. Component failures are most likely to occur during this initial time period.

bus Signal paths, or lines, responsible for moving bits of information from one place to another. In microcomputers, the three buses used are: the address bus, which sends locations of data back and forth; the control bus, which transmits signals that regulate data flow; and the data bus, which carries actual program data.

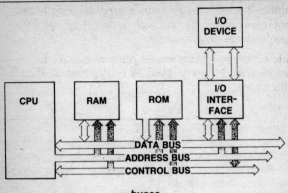

buses

bus driver See driver.

business graphics See graphics, business.

byte A consecutive group of eight bits treated as a unit and often used to represent one character. It is a convenient word length because within it the user is able to express all the important characters needed in an ASCII transmission. See ASCII.

BYTE A popular magazine devoted to the computer market.

C A high-level programming language developed at Bell Laboratories for writing systems software. The popular Unix operating system, also by Bell Labs, was written using the C language. C offers many features that are useful when programming difficult jobs. It helps reduce program length and increases efficiency and was designed for use by professional programmers.

cable connector Male/female plugs necessary for connecting industry-standard cables such as the RS 232.

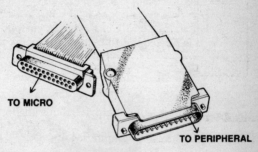

TO MICRO

TO PERIPHERAL

cable connectors

A CAI Computer-Aided Instruction or Computer-Assisted Instruction (acronym).

calculator A data processing device that can perform logical and arithmetic operations, but which has limited user programming capability.

call A control transfer or a branch to a subroutine; the type of subroutine may vary according to the specific needs of the program.

call instruction A type of instruction that, after diverting execution to a new sequence of instructions, permits a return to the program's original sequence.

calling sequence The set of instructions that serves as a linkage going to and returning from program subroutines.

B CAM Content Addressed Memory (acronym). The capability to retrieve data identified by content rather than by numbered location or by an identifiable data pattern.

cancel To stop or abort a command or procedure in progress or pending execution.

CANCL A status word that indicates a deletion of information by a remote computing system.

canned software Packaged software that has been designed for a specific application but is general enough to serve the needs of many users interested in that application. Contrast with custom software, which is developed to serve the specific needs of one user.

card A printed circuit board.

card cage A frame or rack inside the computer housing that holds the printed circuit boards.

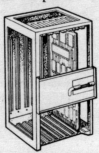

card cage

card reader A device that can transcribe punched-hole data from paper cards into electrical impulses for input into computer memory.

card reader

carriage return A nonprintable character that: (1) causes the cursor of a cathode ray tube screen, or head of a printer, to return to the beginning of the line; (2) is used as a delimiter, signifying the end of a command line, typically referred to as < CR >.

cassette interface The special circuitry used to control data transfer between a cassette tape recorder and a computer.

cassette recording, audio A recording of analog signals representing continuous tones.

catalog (1) An ordered set of items, such as files or programs, arranged in an easy-to-reference structure. (2) To index a set of items, such as a list of files. (3) Same as directory.

catenate See concatenate.

cathode ray tube (CRT). A technology similar to the television set but used for display purposes. The term CRT usually refers to the computer terminal, which includes the screen and keyboard. The screen consists of a vacuum tube with an electron gun that generates and focuses a beam of electrons to a small cross-sectional area on a luminescent screen. The beam's position can be varied, and its intensity

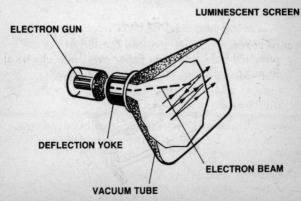

cathode ray tube

adjusted, to produce a visible pattern on the screen. See raster scan; RGB monitor.

C CBASIC A compiler version of the BASIC programming language, designed for use with the 8080 and Z80 family of microprocessors.

A CBBS Computerized Bulletin Board Service (acronym). See electronic bulletin board.

cell A location in memory for one unit of information, typically one character or one byte.

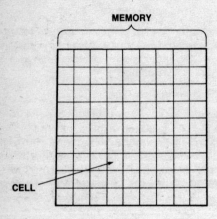

cell

central processing unit (CPU). The main part of a computer system, which contains the Arithmetic-Logic Unit (ALU) and Control Unit (CU).

chained files Data files that consist of a data block series in which the blocks are chained together using forward and backward pointers.

chained list A list in which each item points to the next item; the order of retrieval need not have any relation to the storage order.

chaining (1) The ability of a program to call in another program, or section of a program, to be executed once its own execution has been completed. This allows a program to be larger than would otherwise fit into memory at one time. Sometimes referred to as an overlay. (2) A storage and retrieval system for records that does not require all records to be contiguous.

chaining search A search method in which, by means of a specific identifier, each item that is found has information that leads to the next item in the chain, until either the end of the chain is reached or the desired record is found.

chained sector A storage method that allows one logical unit to be spread across different areas on disk, as opposed to being stored as one contiguous area.

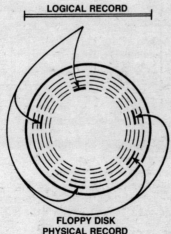

LOGICAL RECORD

FLOPPY DISK
PHYSICAL RECORD

chained sectors

channel Any electronic communication link between two points (transmitter and receiver).

channel adapter A device that enables communication between data channels on different hardware.

character One of a set of symbols, such as letters,

digits, or punctuation marks, that can express information when collectively arranged. Although these symbols are intelligible to humans, they are not understood by computers. For this reason, standardized character codes consisting of groups of binary digits have been developed to allow characters to be machine processed. In most microprocessors, a character is represented by 8 bits, or 1 byte.

character code A code, such as ASCII (American Standard Code for Information Exchange) or ISO (International Standards Organization), that assigns a special standardized group of binary digits to each printed character. See ASCII; ISO.

character pitch In a line of text, the number of characters per inch.

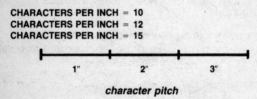

CHARACTERS PER INCH = 10
CHARACTERS PER INCH = 12
CHARACTERS PER INCH = 15

1″   2″   3″

character pitch

character pitch display The ability of a printer to output characters in a number of different pitches (sizes) requested by the software.

character printer An output device which transfers one character to the print medium. The most popular character printers are dot-matrix and daisy wheel types.

character recognition A process allowing a computer to recognize a printed or written symbol or character. The process involves (a) scanning the symbol; (b) encoding the symbol into a square grid format; (c) comparing the encoded symbol against a library of stored symbol templates until the appropriate match is found; (d) substituting the standardized symbol for the recognized symbol.

character recognition

character set The combined group of characters available for inputting or outputting data on a particular computer or peripheral. Some computers allow for alternate character sets such as foreign-language or graphic symbols; others provide for user modification of character sets.

character-size control Ability to view a full page of data at a regular character size or one-half page at double size.

check sum A means of verifying accuracy by summing groups of digits and comparing the result against a previously calculated sum.

chip An integrated circuit etched on a tiny piece of silicon or germanium.

B CIM Computer Output Microfilm (acronym). A system that uses microfilm technology rather than printing on paper.

circuit A connector of electronic devices and wires; electrical current flows through it, and it is used to perform certain types of functions.

circuit capacity Number of channels in a circuit that can be dealt with simultaneously.

clear to send (CTS). An RS 232 standard control signal used in line control sequences to indicate the availability of a data link for transmission in a particular direction.

clipping A program procedure used to avoid unwanted "wrap-around" or the shifting to the side of an

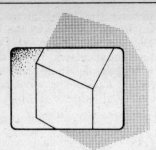

clipping

image too large for the display. A clipping procedure determines which parts of the picture lie outside the screen's boundaries and eliminates those portions.

clock (CLK). A component designed to generate regular pulses in order to synchronize the timing of events within a computer system, such as memory cycles and circuit switching. Also used as a timing device for coordinating synchronous transmissions.

clock rate The frequency at which pulses are generated from a clock.

C **CMOS** Complementary Metal Oxide Semiconductor (acronym). A large-scale integration (LSI) technology that requires low power consumption and is therefore used in portable applications and for battery-assisted memory systems.

coaxial cable A transmission line that has an inner conductor and an outer shield conductor and that is popular for local area networks (LANs) and other forms of transmission.

B **COBOL** COmmon Business Oriented Language (acronym). A high-level programming language. It is particularly useful in business applications because of its Englishlike self-documenting feature and its ease of output formatting.

CODASYL Conference On DAta SYstems Languages (acronym). A committee developed by the U.S. Department of Defense. The CODASYL Committee adopts specifications for standards such as the language COBOL and the data base standard called NETWORK MODEL 1. These have been incorporated into several industry offerings.

code (1) A system of symbolic characters used to represent data. (2) The set of instructions in a computer program.

cold start Starting the system after a crash or when it has not been in use.

collating sequence The order into which various sets of data are merged when they are combined into one.

command Typically, the portion of a computer instruction that specifies what operation is to be performed; e.g., add, GOTO.

Commodore A manufacturer of microcomputer equipment and software.

common storage A portion of memory for each user that holds data or parameters that are accessible to all programs.

compatible software (1) The ability of software to be run on different computers without modification. (2) A feature that enables different application software programs, such as VisiCalc™ or VisiPlot™, to share common conventions and rules so that they can be used together.

compiler A program designed to translate high-level language (source program) into machine language (object program). A compiler translates the entire high-level source program into an object program before processor execution begins (compare with interpreter). All high-level programs must either be compiled or interpreted before they can be executed. A compiled program runs more quickly than an interpreted program because the translated code for each statement of the completed version is stored on disk or tape and can be run at any time, while an interpreted version needs to be translated (or retranslated) each time it is run.

composite video See video signal.

CompuServe™ A commercial electronic data base service owned by H. & R. Block, available to computer users on a subscription basis. It offers access to information sources, electronic bulletin boards, electronic mail, and other services. Formerly called MicroNet.

computer-aided instruction (CAI). An educational procedure supported and assisted by computers; this includes electronic tutorials and automated worksheets. Also computer-assisted instruction.

computer graphics The process of delivering to the user pictorial representations of information through information-processing techniques; e.g., graphs, drawings, etc.

computer literacy General learning, knowledge, and fluency with computer terms and computer usage.

computer system A machine and its components that take information in various forms as input and, through logical and mathematical operations, transforms the data into a suitable form either for further processing or for use as is.

concatenate To chain together, to link, or to arrange as a series, retaining the original order within each of the chained items.

conditional branch A transfer of control within a program, dependent on a certain condition being met by either a mathematical or logical operation or a combination of the two.

contention system A "trial and error" technique of transmitting data on a local area network (LAN). If the data channel is free, transmission may occur. If not, the sending station must wait and try at a later time. A contention system permits multiple users without requiring central control.

continuous Pertaining to quantitative variations where by there are no discernible breaks between points of measurement.

continuous-tone image A black and white or color image formed of combinations of separate areas made up of different color tones or gray tones. Contrast with line drawing.

control character (1) A character that initiates some kind of physical control action but is not printed on the output page; e.g., line feed, tab, form feed. (2) A character that turns off a peripheral device or a printer. (3) Sometimes control characters are used in combination with other characters in order to define unique commands; e.g., "CTRL" (control key) and "C" together might tell the system to abort the program.

control information Information sent between devices in order to control their functions.

control key Typically referring to a key on the CRT keyboard that controls some cursor or program function; e.g., move cursor up, move cursor right, branch to a certain program routine. When pressed simultaneously with another key—"CTRL" "Q", for example—special functions such as block moves or deletions may be invoked.

control panel The part of the console that actually contains the controls and indicators.

controller Electronic circuitry, usually a microprocessor, that allows communication between a computer processing unit and a peripheral device.

conversational mode Refers to the communication between a computer and user in which both the computer and human respond. Same as interactive.

coordinate paper A continuous-feed graph paper that is used for printouts produced on a plotting device.

coordinate system A representation of measurement along axes (intersecting lines); it is used to create graphs showing computation results or comparisons.

coprocessor An auxiliary processor devoted exclusively to time-consuming tasks (e.g., floating point arithmetic) in order to free the central processing unit (CPU), resulting in faster execution. In some setups, this type of chip is used to emulate a different computer.

copy holder A unit for holding papers so they can be easily read by the user while typing on a keyboard. Same as data holder.

copy holder (or data holder)

core A storage technology that was used in older computers before semiconductor memory became popular. Core is a nonvolatile high-speed storage that consists of tiny magnetic "donuts." These units can retain either a positive or negative charge to represent digital information.

courseware Computer programs used in teaching environments.

A CPM Critical Path Method (acronym).

A **CP/M™** Same as CP/M-80.

A **CP/M-80™** Control Program for Microcomputers (acronym). An operating system developed by Digital Research, Inc. for the Intel 8080 and Zilog family of 8-bit word-size microprocessors.

A **CP/M-86™** Control Program for Microcomputers (acronym). An operating system developed by Digital Research, Inc. for the Intel 8086/8088 16-bit (refers to word size) family of microprocessors. It was derived from the CP/M-80. (See preceding entry.)

C **CP/NET** CP/M NETwork (acronym).

A **cps** characters per second (acronym).

A **CPU** Central Processing Unit (acronym).

CPU handshaking Interaction between a CPU and peripheral devices or, in some cases, between the CPU and users.

CPU time The amount of time needed for an operation to be completed.

crash The condition of a system that has become unusable; the cause may be either a hardware malfunction or a software problem.

A **CR** Carriage Return (acronym). Also "ENTER."

A **CRC** Cyclic Redundancy Check (acronym). A bit check that is used to detect incorrect transmission of data. The data have a mathematical operation performed on them at the sending end. The operation is repeated at the receiving end so the two can be compared.

Critical Path Method (CPM). A technique that defines a project in terms of its component events. By ordering the events and showing their interdependencies, this method allows the user to isolate the critical events, whose delay might delay overall completion of the project. These events are said to lie on the critical path. A diagram maps

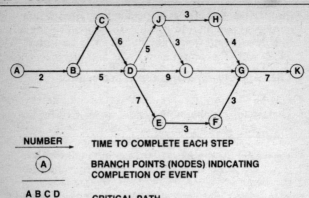

NUMBER → TIME TO COMPLETE EACH STEP

(A) → BRANCH POINTS (NODES) INDICATING
COMPLETION OF EVENT

ABCD → CRITICAL PATH

critical path method

parallel "paths" along a time scale in order to
show the "critical path" of those functions that, if
delayed, would postpone the entire project. Those
functions that may have "slack" may also be
identified.

B CROM <u>C</u>ontrol <u>R</u>ead <u>O</u>nly <u>M</u>emory (acronym). The
storage area in a CPU that is set aside for
microinstructions that, when grouped together, form
procedures such as branch, add, etc.

A CRT <u>C</u>athode <u>R</u>ay <u>T</u>ube (acronym).

CRT terminal A cathode ray tube screen for display
of data combined with a keyboard for data input.
See cathode ray tube; keyboard.

cryptographic Pertaining to a system for coding data
in order to conceal its meaning.

crystal A quartz crystal that, due to its piezoelectric

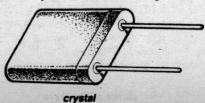

crystal

properties, vibrates at a specific frequency when energy is supplied to it. The vibrations provide a highly accurate frequency by which to time the clock within a computer system. See piezoelectric.

CTRL Abbreviation for control. See control character.

A **CTS** <u>C</u>lear <u>To</u> <u>S</u>end (acronym).

A **CU** <u>C</u>ontrol <u>U</u>nit (acronym).

cursor (1) A special character on the video display (e.g., a triangle, rectangle, or cross) that indicates the next position at which a character will be entered or deleted. It is moved about the screen by program commands or by a designated key or other input device. (2) An input device used with a digitizer tablet. See digitizer, cross-haired cursor; graphics tablet.

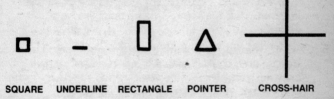

SQUARE   UNDERLINE   RECTANGLE   POINTER   CROSS-HAIR

cursors

cursor control keys Specifically designated keys on the keyboard used to change the position of the cursor on the display screen.

cursor control keys

cursor positioning Describes the action of moving the cursor in different directions: up, down, right, left, home (upper left corner of screen), bottom of screen, etc.

cursor tracking Controlling a cursor on a graphics display by moving a stylus on a graphics tablet connected to the terminal. See graphics tablet.

cursor tracking

curve follower A peripheral device that will read data represented on a graph.

custom software Programs designed by special order to serve a user's specific requirements. Usually more costly than packaged or canned software.

cybernetics The field of science involved in comparative study of the automatic control of, regulation of, and communication between machine and man. These studies include comparisons between information-handling machines and the brains and nervous systems of animals and humans.

cycle stealing The use of slack time in a processor's instruction cycle for operations other than the normal execution of program instructions; e.g., execution of input/output requests from a disk drive or terminal controller.

cycle time The time required by a computer system to complete any specific function. This includes the elapsed time interval, beginning at the moment information is called for from a storage location or device, through the time at which the information is made available and the device completes its internal cycle to become ready for use again.

D

A D <u>D</u>ata (acronym).

D/A <u>D</u>igital to <u>A</u>nalog (acronym). The act of converting digital electrical signals (individual, separate units) from the computer into analog (continuous) signals, such as voltage, sound, etc., in order to drive external devices (such as a music synthesizer) that require analog input.

daisy wheel A type of print element used in some letter-quality printers. It is shaped like a wheel with radial spokes; each spoke has a single raised character on the end. As the wheel turns, the

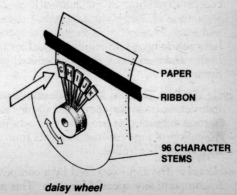

PAPER

RIBBON

96 CHARACTER STEMS

daisy wheel

spokes are impacted by a tiny hammer. This type of printer offers better print quality than a dot-matrix printer but at a higher cost.

data Information that is input to a computer system and is then processed by mathematical and logical operations so that, ultimately, it can be output in a sensible form. It usually consists of numbers, facts, letters, or systems that refer to or describe an object, idea, condition, situation, relationship, or other type of information.

data base An organization of data files containing information or reference material on a particular subject or subjects. It is typically structured so that headings or keywords can be referenced easily, which allows efficient and simple access to and retrieval of records. The individual files are further structured into a hierarchy of records and fields.

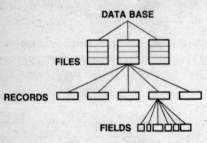

data base

data chaining A technique in which parts of records are stored in areas that are not contiguous but are referenced as a whole by each record having the ability to call the next.

data channel A two-way link for communication between two points.

data communications The technology covering the transfer of computer-encoded information from one point to another by means of various transmission systems.

data communications equipment (DCE). The equipment associated with transmission of data from one point to another. An example would be a modem used to link a computer to a remote terminal, accomplished by connection to a phone line.

data compression (1) Saving storage space by elimination of gaps, redundancies, unnecessary data, or empty fields. (2) Display techniques that reduce time and effort when examining whole data records.

data file A group of records with common descriptive attributes. For example, a customer data file might consist of records describing basic customer information. Each record would represent one customer of the company.

data holder Same as copy holder.

data link The physical communications path used for information transmission between two points.

Datapro™ A research service company that provides in-depth research and information about products and suppliers of hardware and software systems. Their consultants aid managers and supervisors in purchasing equipment and software.

data processing The input, storage, manipulation, and dissemination of information using sequences of mathematical and logical operations.

data reduction Transformation of raw (unprocessed, crude) data into a more useful condition by statistical methods designed to cull, smooth, or order it or otherwise improve its accuracy or arrangement.

data set A group of data elements that are related.

data sink Any device that can accept data signals from a data transmission device.

data tablet See graphics tablet.

data terminal equipment (DTE). Any piece of communication equipment that sends or absorbs data.

A **DBMS** Data Base Management System (acronym). Application software designed to organize data so that they can be quickly filed in/or retrieved.

A **DCE** Data Communications Equipment (acronym).

A **DDP** Distributed Data Processing (acronym). Decentralized computer power arranged by hooking two or more processors together in a network so that each CPU is not tied up with processing information not related to its specific function.

dead halt A halt situation in which the system cannot return to the point at which it stopped. Same as drop-dead halt.

debugger Systems software designed to aid the programmer in discovering problems found during routine testing of software. Debuggers usually provide breakpoints and allow user examination of the contents of registers and memory locations.

debugging Trouble-shooting, isolating, and removing errors or malfunctions (bugs) from a computer or a computer program to improve its accuracy or to restore its operation.

debugging suppression Suppression of printing of repetitions of the same bug in a program. Only the first occurrence of a bug in a loop will be printed out for examination.

B **DEC** Digital Equipment Corporation (acronym). Manufacturers of early computers and a variety of contemporary mini- and microcomputer systems.

decode (1) To determine the meaning of a set of signals that describe an operation or an instruction to be executed. (2) To apply a code that reverses a previous encoding.

decoder A device that translates a set of coded signals.

decrement To decrease a variable or a counter by a fixed quantity.

dedicated channel or line A link used for communication between devices whose function is solely devoted to serving those devices. Typically, a dedicated line is leased from some carrier such as the phone company. Therefore, no one else but the lessee will be able to use that line. This is in contrast to a dial-up line where one only has "ownership" of the line for as long as the connection is made.

dedicated system A computer system designed for a primary application such as word processing or graphics. Additional applications may be possible with supplementary components and software.

default value Values supplied by the computer system itself when no explicit value is received from the program or user.

degausser A device designed to demagnetize a magnetic tape. Also bulk eraser.

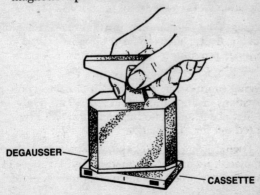

DEGAUSSER

CASSETTE

degausser

degradation testing Measuring the performance of a system at its extreme limits of operation.

delimiter A marker character that is used to limit the bounds of a group of related characters in a program but is not considered a member of the group. A character, a return, a comma, or a slash may be inserted as a delimiter.

demodulate To turn an analog signal back into a digital one.

depth queuing In a two-dimensional projection of a three-dimensional object (pseudo 3-D), using techniques to enhance the three-dimensional appearance of the subject. Examples are perspective, shading, and making parts of the object meant to appear closer to the viewer brighter than those meant to appear in the distance, since brightness falls off with distance.

descenders The portions of printed or displayed alphabet letters that extend below their base line, including the letters g, j, p, q, and y. Some dot-matrix printers do not form descenders below the letter base line.

descenders

desktop computer A unit with physical dimensions that will fit conveniently on a desktop. See microcomputer; personal computer. Contrast with minicomputer; main frame.

destructive read Destruction of source-input data during a read.

device independence The ability in a program to use input or output regardless of what type of peripheral device is being used.

Diablo™ The name of a Xerox-owned company that manufactures computer systems, peripherals, and their well-known daisy-wheel printers. See daisy wheel.

Dialog™ An information data base retrieval service that provides specific information on many subjects of interest to businesses and individual users via computers. The service, operated by Lockheed Corporation, has over 200 data bases covering approximately 55 million records.

digital computer A computer that processes information expressed as combinations of data that are represented by separate, individual units (discrete data). Sequences of binary code, 0's and 1's, are indicated within the computer as either the presence or absence of voltage (on or off). Contrast with analog computer.

digital recording A technique for recording information as discrete points onto magnetic recording media such as magnetic tapes or disks.

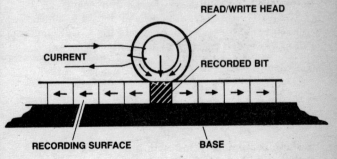

digital recording

digitizer A device that converts analog measurements (such as a drawing) into digital form for input into a digital computer. See graphics tablet.

digitizer, cross-haired cursor A device used to position each point individually, relative to a system of coordinate axes, when inputting data with a digitizer.

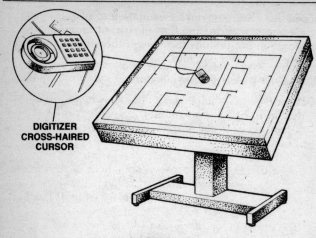

**DIGITIZER
CROSS-HAIRED
CURSOR**

digitizer

digitizer, three-dimensional A digitizing device that
inputs coordinate information directly from a
physical three-dimensional object by means of a
movable arm that measures the dimensions.
Contrast with a two-dimensional digitizer, which
would require scaled drawings of front, side, and
top views of a three-dimensional object as input.

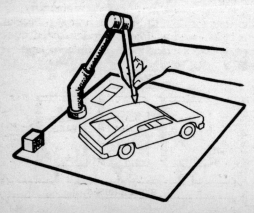

digitizer, 3-D

diode An electronic device composed of two elements; it allows the flow of current in one direction but inhibits the flow in the other direction. Used on chips.

B DIP <u>D</u>ual <u>In</u>-line <u>P</u>ackage (acronym).

B DIP switches A small series of on-off switches on a dual in-line package, enabling user selection of options on a circuit board without hardware alteration.

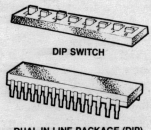

DIP SWITCH

DUAL IN-LINE PACKAGE (DIP)

DIP switch

direct memory access (DMA). An input/output method that allows direct transfer of data between a peripheral input/output device and memory without tying up the computer's central processor. This is a preferred technique for high-speed mass storage devices such as magnetic disks or tape

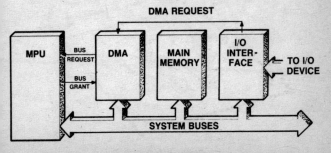

direct memory access

units. Special additional hardware components are required for DMA.

directory The list of all files, which is itself a file, on a computer storage medium for the user's easy reference. Also catalog.

discrete Pertaining to separate, unconnected, distinct parts. Contrast with continuous.

disk crash Failure of a disk, thereby causing the system to malfunction, usually due to destructive contact between the disk drive's read/write head and the surface of the disk.

disk drive A device that rotates magnetic disks and accesses its data by means of a read/write head. Disk drives are operated by disk-drive controllers and utilize the principle of random-access storage.

diskette See floppy disk (also disc).

disk file A file that resides on a magnetic disk.

disk, magnetic A flat, circular storage medium capable of storing digital information. It is organized into a hierarchy of tracks and sectors, allowing information to be read or written via random access. See floppy disk; sectors; tracks.

disk operating system (DOS). An operating system that uses disks for its secondary storage medium. Typically, it regulates space allocation, keeps track of files, saves and retrieves files, and manages other control functions associated with disk storage.

disk pack See hard-disk pack.

disk system All the components required for disk storage, including the disk, disk drive, read/write heads, control electronics and software.

display An output device used for the temporary storage and presentation of graphic and/or alphanumerical data for the purpose of visual examination by the user. The cathode ray tube

(CRT), light-emitting diode (LED), and liquid crystal display (LCD) are display technologies.

display buffer memory The number of characters that can be held in storage for immediate display on the screen.

display highlighting Refers to the way text is emphasized on the screen, using such enhancers as reverse video, underline, blinking, bold, low contrast, and high contrast.

display RAM A RAM area of memory separate from main memory, which stores information to be shown on a video display. The information is not kept in memory once the power is turned off.

distributed data processing See DDP.

dithering With a color display: using a combination of juxtaposed differing colored dots, which in combination will create the illusion of yet another single color. With a black and white display: juxtaposing black dots and white dots in varying ratios so that groups of these dots will create the illusion of a gray scale tone.

A **DMA** Direct Memory Access (acronym).

documentation The set of instructions that accompanies software and hardware to explain their use. Usually in manual form or for display on the CRT screen.

do-loop A command in the FORTRAN language that causes a program segment to be executed repeatedly, with values substituted until certain conditions are satisfied. It then proceeds to the sequence immediately following the loop.

B **DOS** Disk Operating System (acronym).

dot matrix A technique for forming characters by composing them out of selected dots from within a square or rectangular grid pattern of dots (matrix). Common dot matrix sizes for displays and printers are 5 × 7 dots or 7 × 9 dots, but greater numbers of dots can be employed to increase visual clarity (resolution) of the characters.

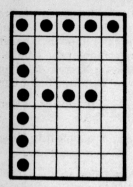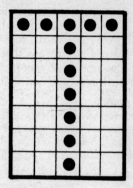

dot-matrix character representation

dot-matrix printer A printer with several tiny projecting wires or needles that combine to form dotted representations of individual characters within a matrix. Dot-matrix printers have poorer image quality than letter-quality printers but type faster and are less costly.

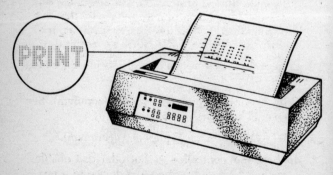

dot-matrix printer

double density A technique used to increase bit density on a magnetic storage medium to twice the amount of single density so that more information can be stored in the same amount of area.

double-precision arithmetic Arithmetic in which the accuracy is doubled by employing twice as many bits (two words) to represent a number. The larger word size means that the computer can handle numbers with more significant figures, enabling greater precision. See word size; significant figures.

double-sided disk A magnetic disk capable of storing information on both of its surfaces.

down load To transfer programs and/or data files from a computer to another device or computer.

down time Time during which a computer is not functional due to mechanical failure or electronic problems. It usually refers to the whole computer system being inoperative rather than just one problem area.

A **DP** Data Processing (acronym).

driver Small programs that are used to control external devices or to run other programs. Driver software directs production, manipulation, and presentation of appropriate signals by the processor so that, at the correct moment, the peripheral device will perform as required.

drop A remote terminal location within a terminal network.

A **DSK** Dvorak Simplified Keyboard (acronym). See Dvorak keyboard.

A **DTE** Data Terminal Equipment (acronym).

dual-channel controller A controller that enables reading from and writing to a device to occur simultaneously.

dual-disk drive A floppy-disk system with two drive mechanisms and recording heads, which allows increased storage capacity and disk-to-disk data transfer and back-up.

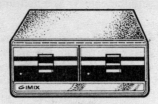

dual-disk drive

dual in-line package (DIP) A standard integrated circuit enclosed in a molded plastic container. It consists of two parallel rows of pins that connect to the circuit board. These circuits are the basic building block of integrated circuit boards.

dual intensity The capability of some printers and display devices to reproduce symbols in both regular and bold-face formats.

dual-mode printer See printer, dual-mode.

dual processors A computer that uses two processors, the second of which could be either a back-up to perform additional functions or to aid in the use of an auxiliary operating system.

dumb (terminal) A terminal that does not have a microprocessor to control various terminal tasks. In contrast, a smart terminal might allow word processing functions to be done utilizing the power of the terminal and not the CPU. A dumb terminal would not have this capability. See smart terminal.

dummy variable Used as an argument for a function or subroutine and whose purpose is to transfer the data from the main program to the function or subroutine.

dump To display, print, or store the contents of the computer's memory.

duplex A method of communicating between two devices that permits data transfer in both directions simultaneously. See half duplex; full duplex.

Dvorak keyboard A keyboard arrangement that is easier and faster to use than the standard QWERTY keyboard. Programs are available to simulate the Dvorak keyboard as an overlay for the standard QWERTY keyboard.

Dvorak keyboard

dynamic printout A situation in which a computer program directly creates its printed output. Because of the greatly disparate speeds of the computer processing unit and the printer, this situation is usually not preferred. In some computers, a buffer enables the printing to occur without limiting the CPU speed. See spooling.

dynamic RAM A type of MOS memory circuit that requires refreshing (internal regeneration of its contents). The advantages are higher density and speed as compared to static RAM; however, additional refresh circuits are necessary.

dynaturtle In the Logo language, a dynamic cursor instead of a static one. The cursor is referred to as a turtle, which is used to produce graphics. Commands to a dynaturtle specify a change in velocity and acceleration during the creation of a drawing. The path of the turtle becomes a line in the drawing.

E

echo The return of a transmitted signal back to its source, with a delay that indicates the signal is a reflection rather than the original.

echo check A method for checking the accuracy of a transmission by reflecting the transmitted data back to its source for comparison. If the data are sent from a display, they go first to the receiver and then show up afterward on the display screen for verification.

edge-card connector A unit that connects printed circuit cards to a mother board or to other devices, such as an input/output device hooked up via cables.

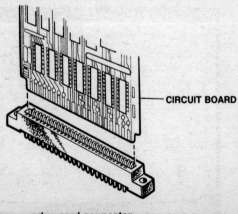

edge-card connector

editor See text editor.

A EDP Electronic Data Processing (acronym).

eight bit Refers to word size. See microprocessor, 8-bit; microcomputer, 8-bit.

electronic bulletin board An electronic call-up service that lets users compose and store messages to be retrieved by other users.

electronic mail Messages sent by one user and retrieved by another through an electronic service system, usually via telephone lines or radio transmission. Each user must know the other's identification number. The mail service is instantaneous.

electronic spreadsheet Software that simulates a business or scientific worksheet in which the user can indicate data relationships. When data are changed, the program has the ability to recalculate instantly any related factors and to save all the information in memory. Such programs often have "Calc" in their names; e.g., VisiCalc™ and SuperCalc™.

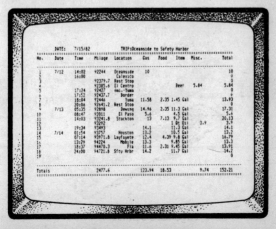

electronic spreadsheet

electrostatic printer A small-format, nonimpact printer that forms characters by putting an electrostatic charge on the character outline, dusting the paper with dry ink, and then melting the ink to form a bond with the paper.

embedded command In word processing, one or more characters inserted into the text that do not print but instruct either the printer or word processing program to carry out a task; e.g., go to half spacing, end the page, etc.

emulate To imitate one system with another system so that the imitation system is perceived to be the same as the original. The modification that occurs affects the hardware, not the software that will be run.

emulator, software Software that gives one computer system (computer B) the ability to execute programs originally written for another computer system (computer A) without changing the hardware or reprogramming the programs that were written for computer A. The program acts on computer B, not on the other programs to be used. However, since the computer must look up the corresponding machine language each time an instruction appears, the resulting runs take longer than normal runs. See emulate.

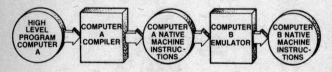

emulator, software

encoder A device that substitutes one set of symbols for another.

end of file (EOF). A marker that indicates the end of a file.

end-of-page indicator A feature that halts the printer

at the end of each completed page of output to allow the user to manually handle paper, ribbon, or font changes.

end of transmission (EOT). A signal indicating that the end of the data transmission has been reached.

end value A value that is used for comparison with a count, index, etc., to see if a certain condition has been met.

ENTER Often used interchangeably with carriage return.

A **EOF** End Of File (acronym).

A **EOM** End Of Message (acronym).

A **EOT** End Of Transmission (acronym).

C **EPROM** Erasable Programmable Read Only Memory (acronym). A programmable memory that, as opposed to RAM (random-access memory), can only be read and normally cannot be changed or written into. However, there is a method by which the chip can be reprogrammed. Using special hardware, an EPROM can be erased with ultraviolet light and reprogrammed.

EPROM programmer A special device used to program EPROM chips.

EPROM programmer

Epson A manufacturer of dot-matrix printers and other microcomputer products.

ergonomics The study of the relationship between the efficiency and comfort involved in human performance when using machines. Also called human factors.

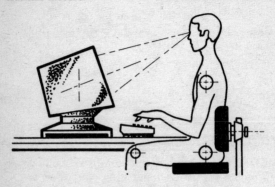

ergonomics

escape (ESC). A nonprinting character used by the terminal and/or host computer, typically in conjunction with another character, to perform a specific function; e.g., "ESC" plus "Y" might tell the terminal that the user is going to move the cursor.

A **ETB** End of Transmission Block (acronym).

Ethernet A local-area network (LAN) system developed by Xerox Corp. Its goal is to become a standard for such applications as office automation and distributed processing.

A **ETX** End of TeXt (acronym).

C **ETX/ACK protocol** End of TeXt/ACKnowledge (acronym). A procedure used in communications to verify transmission.

event A processing action or occurrence that alters data files.

exception-principle system A system that reports only those results that differ from predesignated results or criteria.

exception reporting A record that contains only certain types of results: changes; values that do not match preset criteria; values that exceed previously indicated limits.

exclusive OR (XOR). A Boolean operative whose definition is that the output is 1 only when either (but not both) of the two inputs is 1. See Boolean Algebra.

executable Can be processed, or executed, by the computer without need for translation.

execute To interpret a programmed instruction and perform the indicated operation or operations.

execution time The portion of an instruction cycle during which the actual work is performed or operation is executed; i.e., the time required to decode and perform an instruction.

expander boards Boards that interface to the system and allow the user to add more circuitry for system expansion.

expansion slots Slots for additional circuit boards, found inside the main computer housing, that can be used to expand the system's capabilities through addition of peripheral devices. A board may in itself provide the increased capability (such as a 16K RAM board) or, if a new device is added to the system, a control board is placed in an expansion slot to drive the added unit.

extended-precision arithmetic An operation that yields an answer that is more accurate (with more significant figures) than double-precision arithmetic.

extension See file-name extension.

external memory Same as mass storage.

F

facsimile A process that involves the electronic transmission of images, usually from one system to a remote receiving station. Images are electronically scanned, converted into transmission signals, and then sent to the receiving station. These signals can then be converted at the receiving station to create a duplicate of the original image.

facsimile transceiver A device used to implement facsimile production and transmission.

facsimile transceiver

fan-fold paper Continuous sheets of paper connected with perforations, folded in an accordion fold and used with a printer to provide a continuous feed without operator assistance. Also called Z-fold.

fan-fold paper

fault time Same as down time.

fault-tolerant A system or program capable of correct operation despite a component failure.

A FDC Floppy Disk Controller (acronym).

feedback (1) A response by the system to an input. (2) Use of output as input to either the same or another process.

fetch To retrieve data or instructions from storage.

field An area within a record that stores a particular type of data such as social security numbers, names, addresses, ages, etc. See data base.

CUSTOMER NO. 1 RECORD

ACOMP CO.	110 MAIN ST	RICHMOND	VA	23225	804 531-2057

fields

B FIFO queue First In First Out structure (acronym). The first data item deposited in a queue of data items is to be the first one reached in processing.

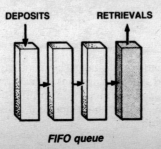

FIFO queue

file A group of organized data (records) assembled for one particular purpose and considered as one unit and stored in permanent off-line storage, such as a disk drive, tape, or disk.

file gap A space at the end of the file that signifies to the system where the file ends.

file-name extension A code, very often of three letters, that forms the second part of a file name and is separated from the file name by a period. This supplement to the name often is used to help differentiate the related files. For example: ORDER.BAS might be a Basic program for order entry; ORDER.SAV might be the executable version of ORDER.BAS; ORDER.DAT might be a data file that holds ORDER data.

file organization The arrangement of files on the storage media.

firmware Programs or data stored in ROM. These are not alterable by software and are not lost when the power is turned off.

fixed-length record file A data file in which each record is of the same length. Contrast with variable-length record file.

fixed-point representation A number notation system in which, typically, numbers are represented as whole integers with the decimal point assumed to be fixed and located to the right of the integer. (In some cases the "fixed point" is located to the left.) Contrast with "floating-point representation."

flag An indicator used in both hardware and software that is associated with a special condition. A software flag is used to inform a later program segment of a specific condition. Flags may be checked at various points in the program for certain conditions. Hardware flags may cause specific events to occur at designated times.

flatbed plotter A plotter that employs plotting heads

that move over a flat surface in both horizontal and vertical directions. Compare with drum plotter, in which heads move in one direction and paper in another.

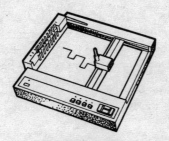

flatbed plotter

flexible-membrane keyboard See membrane keyboard.

flicker In a raster scan display, flicker refers to the actual detection by the human eye of the repeated on-off cycle resulting from the phosphor screen image being regenerated by an electron beam 30 or more times per second.

flip-flop A bistable circuit; i.e., a circuit capable of storing a bit of information and of assuming two stable states (0 and 1) as long as power is applied. Flip-flops may be grouped together to form registers.

floating-point representation A notation system in which the decimal point is not fixed; when representing these numbers in a computer, the symbol typically consists of two parts. One part contains the number's fractional component; the other part is expressed as a power of the base (radix) of the number. For example: standard notation, 0.0000256; scientific notation, 0.256×10^{-4}; floating-point representation, $.256E\text{-}04$.

floppy disk A flexible, flat, circular mylar medium that magnetically records and provides access to

stored data. It is divided into concentric circular
tracks and wedge-shaped sectors. The disk is sealed
in a protective square cover that is lined with a
soft material, which cleans as it rotates. The cover
has several openings and notches to accommodate
the disk drive. Also disc, diskette. See digital
recording; disk, magnetic; read/write head;
sectors; tracks.

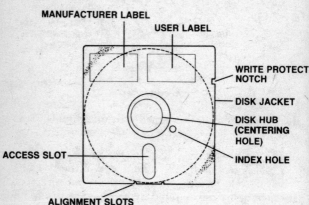

floppy disk

flowchart A graphic representation of the sequences
proposed to solve a problem.

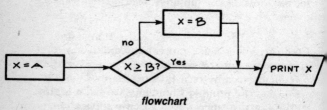

flowchart

flowchart symbols Flowcharts use standardized sets
of symbols to represent operations. Boxes represent
order or computations; diamonds represent tests
and decisions; other shapes are used to represent
input/output, connector points, etc. The symbols

aid in organizing sequences of operations when
writing computer programs.

PROCESSING OPERATION (ARITHMETIC, LOGIC, DATA MOVEMENT)

SUBROUTINE

CONNECTOR ARROWS

INPUT/ OUTPUT

CONNECTOR POINT

DECISION LOGIC

TERMINAL POINT (BEGINNING OR ENDING)

flowchart symbols

font A family or collection of printing characters of a
particular size and style.

format (1) The arrangement of data into a specified
layout. (2) The designated placement of text and
margins and other elements in hard copy. (3)
Programming to set up text arrangements
for outputting.

formatting (1) Setting up the order of the
information that is input to a computer or a
peripheral device. (2) Arranging the layout of the
data that is output from the computer or a
peripheral.

for/next loop A section of code in BASIC that goes
through a fixed number of iterations, based on a
preset index. See do-loop.

FORTH A high-level programming language that
allows the programmer to generate powerful
(efficient) computer commands easily by using
"primitives" (simple statements) to tailor highly
complex instructions to a specific application.
FORTH is characterized by its speed and economy of
memory use.

FORTRAN FORmula TRANslator (acronym). A
high-level language originally developed by IBM
for numerical and scientific applications. One of the

oldest and most popular high-level languages, it is now also used in many commercial and industrial applications. It must always be compiled rather than interpreted.

free format No restrictions are imposed on the format in which the data are entered.

frequency The number of times a recurring signal repeats itself within a given unit of time. Frequency is usually measured as the number of cycles per second. See hertz; MHz.

friction feed In a printer, a method by which paper is moved between the primary roller and the pinch roller (as in a standard typewriter).

full duplex A mode of communications in which two systems can transmit and receive data simultaneously so that two different sets of signals can be sent at the same time.

full-page display A terminal that displays at least 80 columns (80 characters across) and 55 lines of copy (the average 8½ × 11-inch page capacity) on the screen at one time.

full-page display

function codes Codes that help control functions of peripheral devices; e.g., a line feed for a printer would be a function code.

function keys Special keys on the keyboard that can initiate a special function within a program, dependent on how the programmer defines the keys in the program. The key will send a specific code to the program, which will be acted upon by the software.

function keys

A FX Fixed area (acronym). An area on a disk that is protected and that holds certain files and programs.

garbage (1) An accumulation of unwanted, meaningless data that may clutter up storage. (2) Unreliable results of unreliable data that were put back into the computer.

gates An electronic circuit that has several inputs and one output; the output is not acted upon until the input meets certain conditions. In a computer, this is called a "logic circuit," which gives electronic results on the basis of logical function inputs.

giga A prefix used to denote one billion.

B GIGO Garbage In Garbage Out (acronym). A saying that refers to the inability of obtaining good results with bad data.

glitch An undesirable electronic noise or interference that causes errors or failures in a computer system.

global search A program routine that searches for every occurrence of a character, word, or phrase within a text file.

global variable A variable that may be referred to throughout a main program and all of its subroutines, as compared to a local variable that may be referenced only within the specific program segment in which it has been defined.

GOTO (GO TO). A branching instruction in high-level programming languages.

A GPIB <u>G</u>eneral-<u>P</u>urpose <u>I</u>nterface <u>B</u>us (acronym). The name given to the IEEE 488 bus standard. See HPIB.

graceful exit The ability of the user to exit from a program without having to turn off the machine.

graphics, business Refers to various types of graphs and charts that represent sales, profits, losses, inventory, and similar concepts. Examples are bar graphs, scatter graphs, and pie graphs.

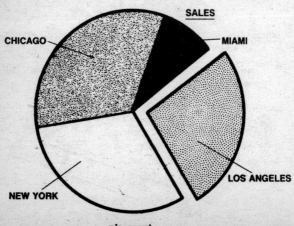

pie graph

UNIT SALES TERRITORY No. 1

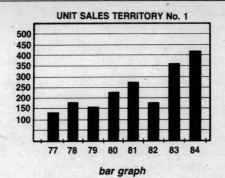

bar graph

graphics solution The result of problem solving, put into a visual form for clarity.

graphic tablet A popular type of digitizing device that utilizes a flat tablet and a stylus for graphic input. Existing drawings can be traced or new drawings created by moving the stylus across the tablet, which records the stylus position relative to an X-Y coordinate system and inputs this information into the system. The image that is being created will appear simultaneously on a connected display screen. The tablet may have a menu of predefined specialized graphic symbols that can be chosen and used as an aid in creating drawings. The tablet provides an efficient method of converting object shapes into computer storable information. See digitizer; cursor tracking; stylus.

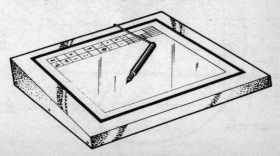

graphics tablet

graphics, three-dimensional See line drawing, three-dimensional.

graphics, two-dimensional See line drawing, two-dimensional.

gray scale images A hierarchy of solid continuous blocks of single tones that can be combined in different sizes and shapes to form or to represent an image. In its most sophisticated form, a sufficient number of gray scale tones can be combined and interpolated to form an image emulating a standard, continuous-tone, black and white photograph.

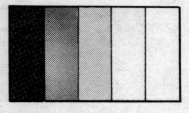

gray scale

group indicate The first record of a group is used in order to indicate information about the contents of the group.

gulp A slang term for a group of bytes.

hacker Computer jargon for a person who is intensely interested in and/or very knowledgeable about computer hardware.

half-duplex When transmission is capable of being sent in only one direction at a time.

half-height floppy-disk drives A design that allows a floppy-disk drive to displace approximately one-half the physical space required by a traditional floppy-disk drive.

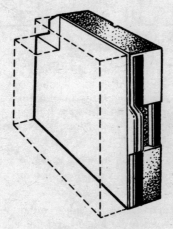

half-height floppy disk

halt The situation in which the computer system stops processing in the middle of a program, often in response to a particular instruction.

handheld computer A system small enough to carry in a pocket. Contrast with portable computer and desktop computer.

hands-on The act of physically using a computer.

handshaking A term that refers to the communication of control information between the system components. For example, one component will request another component to perform some function; when the component is ready to carry out that function, it will notify the original component.

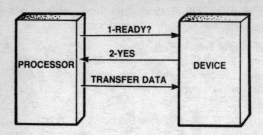

handshaking

hang-up The computer system stops forward progress in the program and is for all practical purposes "halted" even though the machine is still running. For example, an infinite loop can cause the system to become "hung" even though the program is still running. See halt.

hard copy Output of information in permanent form, usually on paper, as opposed to temporary display on a CRT screen.

hard-disk cartridge A cartridge containing a rigid disk designed to be loaded and unloaded into a hard-disk system.

hard-disk cartridge

hard-disk cylinder A term that refers to the same track on all of the platters in a hard-disk pack, producing a vertical stack of tracks that form a cylinder. A cylinder is created after a track has been filled when, in order to minimize head movements during access, subsequent records are allocated to the same track position on the disk directly underneath or above the original track.

This allocation strategy cuts down on time needed to retrieve data.

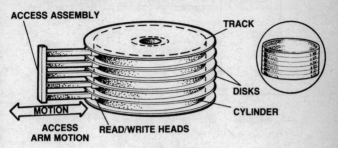

hard-disk cylinder

hard-disk pack A removable set of magnetic disks loaded as a unit on a disk drive.

hard-disk pack

hard-disk system The hardware needed in order to

hard-disk system

interface hard disks for data and program storage. Compared to floppy-disk systems, hard-disk systems have faster access times, higher capacity, and greater reliability.

hard error An error caused by some malfunction in the hardware; e.g., a disk head reading the information on the disk incorrectly.

hard-sector disk A floppy disk that is divided into sectors and tracks by physical, nonalterable means such as a hole punched in the disk to designate each sector. See soft sector.

hardware The physical components of a computer system: central processor, memory, disk drives, printer, terminal, computer boards, peripherals, etc. Contrast with software and firmware.

head A small electromagnetic device that reads, records, and erases data on a magnetic storage medium such as a disk or recording tape. Also called a "read/write" head. See digital recording.

head crash For disk systems, an unwanted physical contact of the read/write head against the magnetic disk surface and subsequent damage to the disk as a result. See also disk crash.

Heath/Zenith A manufacturer and distributor of computer systems, kits, and electronic products.

hello program The program that is first run in some systems when the machine is started and which allows the user to sign on.

HELP A function available on many systems, it can make available to the user information on points that need further explanation.

hertz (Hz). A measurement of frequency in which one hertz equals one cycle per second. Named for the physicist Heinrich Hertz.

heuristic A trial-and-error method of obtaining a solution to a problem. Contrast to algorithmic.

Hewlett-Packard Manufacturer of a wide range of computer systems.

B HEX <u>HEX</u>adecimal (acronym).

hexadecimal A base 16 number system. The ten decimal digits of 0 to 9 are employed to express the first ten digits of the 16-digit system. A,B,C,D,E, and F are usually used to express the remaining six digits from 10 to 15. The system is used extensively with microcomputers because two hexadecimal symbols can consistently represent 1 byte (8 bits) of binary data, affording a compact system of notation up to a numerical value of 255.

hidden line In a graphic display of a three-dimensional object in line form, the line (or edge), which would be obscured from the viewer's sight by the mass of the object itself, is visible as a result of the projection. Additional routines must be implemented to remove these "hidden lines."

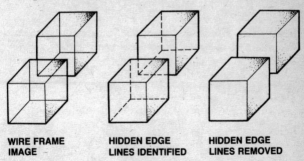

WIRE FRAME IMAGE   **HIDDEN EDGE LINES IDENTIFIED**   **HIDDEN EDGE LINES REMOVED**

hidden line

high-level language Programming languages designed so users can write instructions in Englishlike statements rather than in machine language. One high-level statement translates to several machine-language statements. A compiler or interpreter must be used for this translation. Examples of high-level languages include FORTRAN, BASIC, Pascal, and PL/1.

high resolution Refers to the quality and accuracy of detail that can be represented by a graphics system such as a video display or a printer. Resolution quality depends on the number of basic image-forming units (pixels) within a given area; the greater the number, the higher the resolution.

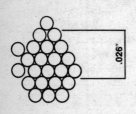
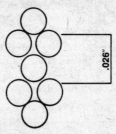

HIGH RESOLUTION TUBE   **CONVENTIONAL TV TUBE RESOLUTION**

high resolution tube

B HITS Hobbyist's Interchange Tape Standard (acronym). A data recording format using tape cassettes; the standard format was designed to allow interchangeability of cassettes and programs.

A HLL High-Level Language (acronym).

A HOL High-Order Languages (acronym). See high-level language.

hold instruction An instruction that causes information to be retained in its original storage area even after it has been copied in another location due to a transfer instruction.

home A command from a program or key on the keyboard that moves the cursor to the starting point of the screen, usually the upper left-hand corner.

homebrew Refers to early computers made by hobbyists (often in their garages), which gave rise to the personal computer and the entire resulting industry.

horizontal scrolling Ability of the system to shift horizontally blocks of lines of text or data in order to view more characters than can fit on the screen at one time.

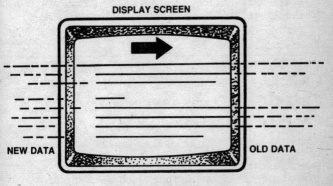

horizontal scrolling

hostile environment The practice of applying software to a system for which it was not designed, using special utilities to make the software and the system compatible.

A HPIB <u>H</u>ewlett-<u>P</u>ackard <u>I</u>nterface <u>B</u>us (acronym). One of a number of standards for connection of hardware. Also called the general-purpose interface bus (GPIB).

human engineering The theory and application of designing in order to serve people, as opposed to designing for a machine. See ergonomics.

Hz <u>H</u>ertz (acronym).

A IBM International Business Machines (acronym).

A IBM PC™ IBM Personal Computer (acronym).

A IC Integrated Circuit (acronym).

idle characters Characters used in data communication to synchronize the transmission.

idle time The period during which a system, or part of a system, is not being used due to lack of demand. For example, the printer could be in use, but the central processing unit could have idle time.

IEEE Institute of Electrical and Electronic Engineers (acronym). Referred to as I-triple-E.

IF-THEN-ELSE A programming instruction that specifies a set of instructions to be carried out under certain conditions. For example, in "if X = 0," then X = 0, is the condition that determines what will occur next, and the computer will be directed to branch to the appropriate statement.

image processing A method of inputting two-dimensional images to a computer and then enhancing or analyzing the imagery into a form that will be more meaningful to the user. Examples include enhancement of drawings for animation, photographs, or computer-aided design models.

impact printer A printer in which a hammer or striking unit transfers ink from ribbon to paper.

These include band, drum, chain, cylinder, type ball, daisy wheel, and thimble design printers. See printer.

implement To carry out or give physical, functional reality to a theory or plan. Various types of software are the tools for implementing usable applications of mathematical, logical, or business theory.

implementation The procedures involved in installing and testing hardware and software in computer systems.

increment (1) As a verb, to increase an integer by a specified amount. (2) As a noun, the amount by which the integer is increased.

indexed sequential access method See ISAM.

information word A word that conveys computer information rather than an instruction.

inhibiting input Input that in some way inhibits production of output.

initialization (1) A process that is carried out at the beginning of a program. It sets all starting values within the system to the prescribed conditions needed for use. (2) A procedure carried out when a disk is first used. It is done only once per disk, not each time the disk is used. The disk is reinitialized only when the user desires to clear out all the old files and start with a blank slate. Disk initialization carries out these steps: (a) enters DOS onto disk; (b) enters the program that runs each time the disk is booted; (c) defines the sectors; (d) establishes the volume table of contents.

ink-jet printer A type of printer in which dot-matrix characters are formed by ink droplets electrostatically aimed at the paper surface. Some advantages are high resolution, color reproduction (if color is used), and quiet operation.

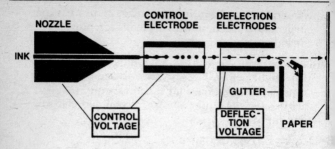

ink-jet printer

in-line subroutine A subroutine that is inserted into the main routine as many times as it is needed.

input/output The processes involved in transferring information into or out of a central processing unit.

input/output processor (IOP). An auxiliary processor dedicated (used for this one purpose only) to controlling I/O transfers, which frees the central processing unit (CPU) for other tasks.

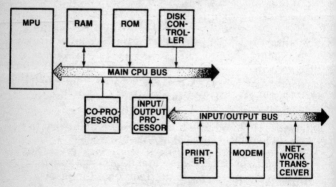

input/output processor

instruction A single operation to be executed by the computer. Instructions may move data, perform arithmetic and logical functions, control I/O devices, etc. A sequence of instructions forms a program.

instruction cycle The time necessary to process a program instruction. This includes fetching, decoding, and execution.

instruction set A means of describing the basic capabilities of a CPU, usually a listing of all the types of instructions a CPU can execute; i.e., arithmetic, data movement, decision and control, and input/output.

INT INTerrupt (acronym).

integer A whole number, one with no fractional parts.

integrated circuit A group of interconnected components fabricated on a tiny chip of silicon. The components form a functioning electronic circuit.

INTEL Corp. Manufacturers of microprocessors, including the INTEL 8080, 8086, and 8088.

intelligent terminal A terminal with microprocessor control. See dumb (terminal).

interactive The ability of the system to handle immediate-response communications between the user and the machine. See user interaction.

interest worlds Areas of special interest for which the computer can serve as a tool or laboratory; some examples are art, music, mathematics, physics, or language.

interface The hardware and/or software necessary to connect one system or device to another.

interlaced field A technique found in raster scan display systems to minimize flicker on the display screen.

interpret To translate a higher-level language program into a program that the machine understands.

interpreter A program designed to translate high-level language instructions (source code) into binary machine code (object code). An interpreter translates each individual high-level statement into object code and executes it before reaching the next statement. Once the statement has been executed, its object code is discarded, and that statement must be retranslated if it is encountered again. This can be time consuming, particularly in loop conditions. Therefore, interpreted programs tend to run more slowly than compiled programs, where all the statements are translated before execution begins, and retranslation of the same statement is not necessary. See compiler.

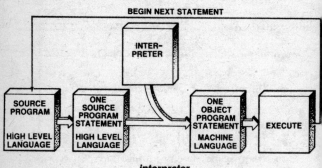

interpreter

interrupt When an input/output device needs to use the CPU for processing, it sends a service request signal to the central processing unit (CPU). When accepted, the CPU halts (interrupts) its current process, saves its contents, and branches to the appropriate I/O routine to service that I/O device. Once the service has been completed, the CPU returns to the process it was involved in before the interrupt or to the interrupt request that is next in priority.

intraoffice network See local-area network.

A I/O Input/Output (acronym).

I/O bound Describes a situation in which the speed of a program or computation is limited by the

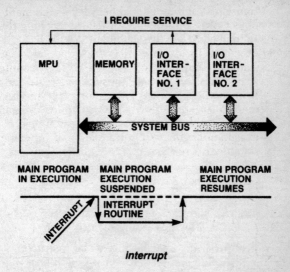

interrupt

capabilities of the input/output devices and/or interfaces. For example, a central processing unit that operates in one-billionth of a second must wait for a printer that operates in one-tenth of a second. See idle time; processor bound.

A IOCS Input/Output Control System (acronym).

A IOP Input/Output Processor (acronym).

B ISAM Indexed Sequential Access Method (acronym). A procedure for storing and retrieving data. It uses a set of indexes (like the table of contents in a book) that describes where the records are on the disks. Each record has "key" information, such as a customer name, that is used to retrieve the whole record.

A ISO International Standards Organization (acronym). An international agency with functions similar to ANSI in the United States, responsible for developing standards for information exchange, such as character codes.

iteration A repetition of one or more statements in a
program, such as a sequence of statements in a
do-loop.

I-triple-E See IEEE.

job A program and data, or group of programs and
data, organized for processing by a computer.

job control program Specifies particular instructions
to the operating system stating the conditions
needed to run a job; i.e., input/output
requirements, etc.

joystick A vertical stick or lever that can be tilted in
various directions to indicate direction of cursor
movement on a screen. Most joysticks can move the
cursor only vertically and horizontally.

joystick

jump Same as branch.

jumper selectible An option on hardware that allows the user, typically through use of a DIP switch, to change various characteristics of the hardware.

jumper tester A device that can test whether or not the assorted options of a device are functioning.

jumper tester

junk Garbled data, most often referring to signals received in communications.

justification Spacing of text or graphics to produce an even, vertically aligned right- or left-hand margin.

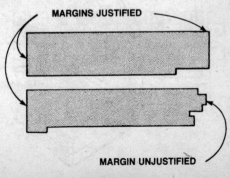

MARGINS JUSTIFIED

MARGIN UNJUSTIFIED

justification

K

A K Kilo (acronym).

A KB KiloBytes (acronym).

key (1) A field or concatenation of fields within a
record, utilized in identifying an item or record
for access purposes. (2) An individual button of a
keyboard used to generate a code to represent a
character.

keyboard An input device consisting of switches
with marked keytops that, when pressed manually,
generate a code representing individual
characters. See ASCII keyboard; QWERTY
keyboard.

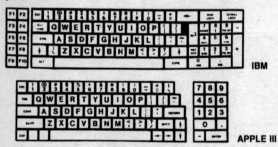

keyboards

keyboard processor A processor used in the keyboard
to determine the active key position, to look up a
corresponding character code in memory (keyboard
ROM), and to place the appropriate code on the
data bus.

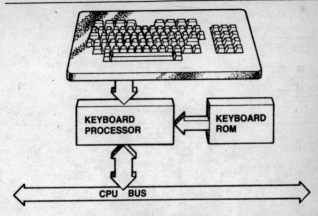

keyboard processor

keyboard ROM A small ROM (Read-Only Memory) in the keyboard that contains standardized character-code tables used by the keyboard processor so that the appropriate code can be looked up on the data bus.

keypad Usually a small group of keys set up for a special purpose, such as the numerical keys to the right of the QWERTY keyboard.

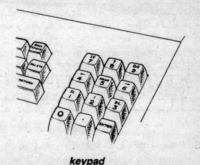

keypad

keypunch A device that records information by punching holes in cards to represent letters, digits, and special characters.

key stations The number of terminals used for data input on a multiple-user system.

key switch The actual switch part of a key—the input key on a keyboard. The most commonly used is a leaf contact-type switch, which yields high-speed operation.

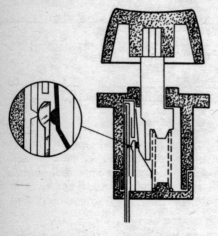

key switch

Kilo A prefix often used to represent 1,000. In the context of computer use, it does not exactly equal 1,000 but refers to 1,024—or 2^{10}—which is a convenient binary approximation of 1,000. A 1K byte memory storage has 1,024 bytes; a 64K byte memory has 65,536 bytes. A 4K chip is a 4,096-bit chip. When not used in reference to a chip, it usually indicates the number of bytes; when used in terms of a chip, the number refers to bits.

kilobaud One thousand bits per second.

B KWIC Key Word In Context (acronym). A permuted index (one that offers lists of titles with each of the major words as the first word and the rest of the words following) that utilizes key words or phrases.

A LAN <u>L</u>ocal <u>A</u>rea <u>N</u>etwork (acronym). See network, local area.

language An intermediate step that allows humans to communicate with a computer. Arbitrary syntax and vocabulary are used to express efficiently particular relationships and to solve specific types of problems.

large scale integration (LSI) A process for fabricating integrated circuits that have thousands of semiconductors such as diodes and transistors (approximately 20,000) on a single silicon chip. See very large scale integration.

laser printers A printer technology that focuses laser beams to form images on photosensitive drums in a principle similar to that used in xerographic office copiers. Laser printers are now used as output devices for computers. They are high speed, high quality, and have relatively high first costs compared to other printer technologies.

A LCD <u>L</u>iquid-<u>C</u>rystal <u>D</u>isplay (acronym). A display technology often used in pocket- and briefcase-sized

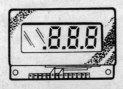

LCD

calculators and computers, as well as wrist watches, because of its thin profile. It features high visibility in high illumination levels but has no visibility in low illumination levels.

least significant bit The bit in the right-most position of a binary word or byte, which is the bit that could be eliminated with the least damage to the precision of the operation. See significant figures; most significant bit.

A LED <u>L</u>ight-<u>E</u>mitting <u>D</u>iode (acronym). A display device technology that has high visibility in low illumination levels and low visibility in high illumination levels.

LED

letter-quality printer A printer that uses a ball, daisy wheel, or thimble element to produce one complete character representation with each stroke. It produces a print image similar to that of a traditional typewriter. Also "line quality" printer. Contrast with dot-matrix printer.

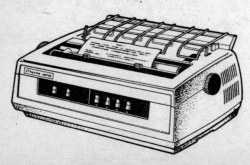

letter-quality printer

library A collection of programs or routines that are used frequently by application programs or system programs. For example, if five users frequently use the same routine, such as a square root function, then one copy of the routine is put into a "library" and accessed as needed instead of each user having to program a square-root function every time it is wanted.

library case A container, usually made of plastic, for storing and protecting floppy disks.

library case

B LIFO stack <u>L</u>ast <u>I</u>n <u>F</u>irst <u>O</u>ut (acronym). A technique for organizing data so that the last entry placed in a stack of data items will be the first entry item to be retrieved. Same as push-down stack.

LIFO stack

light pen A stylus-shaped photosensitive pointing device that allows interactive communication between a computer user and a terminal screen. When the user touches the pen to a position on the screen, then that coordinate on the screen is input as data to the system.

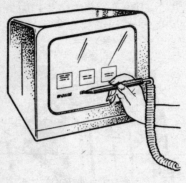

light pen

line coordination Determining whether devices at both ends of a communication line are ready to talk.

line drawing Representation of an object's image by entering a solid-line outline of surfaces. The mass or shape of the form between the lines will be inferred by the viewer. Contrast with continuous-tone image.

line drawing, three-dimensional Describes a three-

line drawing, 3-D

dimensional object's projection onto a two-dimensional display surface. Techniques of perspective projection are employed, similar to the projection of a real object through a lens onto the flat viewing glass of a camera.

line drawing, two-dimensional A method of display that represents line drawings of a flat image, such as a building floor plan or a two-axes graph. No depth is suggested.

line feed A mechanism, control, code, or character that causes paper in a printer to advance one line or the cursor on a CRT screen to move down one line.

line height The height of one line of type measured by the number of lines per inch.

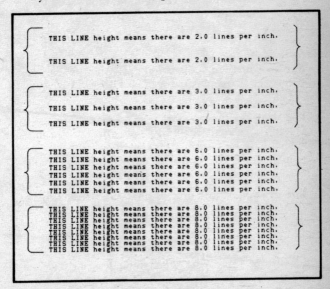

THIS LINE height means there are 2.0 lines per inch.

THIS LINE height means there are 2.0 lines per inch.

THIS LINE height means there are 3.0 lines per inch.

THIS LINE height means there are 3.0 lines per inch.

THIS LINE height means there are 3.0 lines per inch.

THIS LINE height means there are 6.0 lines per inch.
THIS LINE height means there are 6.0 lines per inch.
THIS LINE height means there are 6.0 lines per inch.
THIS LINE height means there are 6.0 lines per inch.
THIS LINE height means there are 6.0 lines per inch.
THIS LINE height means there are 6.0 lines per inch.

THIS LINE height means there are 8.0 lines per inch.
THIS LINE height means there are 8.0 lines per inch.
THIS LINE height means there are 8.0 lines per inch.
THIS LINE height means there are 8.0 lines per inch.
THIS LINE height means there are 8.0 lines per inch.
THIS LINE height means there are 8.0 lines per inch.
THIS LINE height means there are 8.0 lines per inch.
THIS LINE height means there are 8.0 lines per inch.

line height

line printer A printer that produces one full line of type at a time (contrast with character

printer) and operates at a very high speed.
Some line printers can output up to 3,000 or more
lines per minute (lpm).

line-quality printer See letter-quality printer.

line surge A sudden high-voltage condition that can
damage equipment that does not have surge
protection.

linear programming A means of finding the best
possible solution to a problem that is expressed as a
series of linear equations. The solution must
satisfy restrictions that are imposed on the variables
being considered.

linking loader A program designed to link separately
compiled program modules together into one
consecutive memory configuration for execution.
Also link editor.

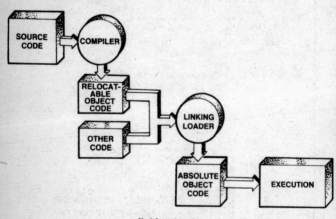

linking loader

B LISP <u>LIS</u>t <u>P</u>rocessing (acronym). An interpretive
programming language whose instructions are
organized to define data relationships through use of
pointers and tree structures. The type of problems
dealt with in artificial intelligence lend themselves
to this kind of organization.

list A set of items structured in a predesignated, logical order.

list processing Methods for processing data that are in list form. Usually, priority is given to techniques such as chaining, altering the logical order of items without changing their physical locations in memory.

local-area network (LAN). See network, local-area.

location The memory cell in which a data word or instruction is stored.

logical record A unit of information containing a group of related fields, all of which are related to a specific computer application. However, the physical storage of the data need not correspond to the logical arrangement. The operating system assembles the separate components. No one particular location is inferred. For example, all information on a customer might be stored in different areas on disk, but together form a logical record. Contrast with physical record.

logic chart See flowchart.

logic gate A component or circuit capable of performing a logic operation. See Boolean Algebra; AND; OR; NOR; NAND.

THIS IS THE SYMBOLIC REPRESENTATION OF AN "AND" LOGIC GATE, AS IT WOULD APPEAR ON COMPUTER SCHEMATICS. SEE SCHEMATIC SYMBOLS.

logic gate

logic theory The science that takes into account logical operations, which are the basis of computer operations. This simulation of simple logic uses electronic circuits to test hypotheses, which are indicated as either true or false by "on" or "off" in the electronic circuit. See Boolean Algebra.

Logo A programming language and a language for learning programming, it was developed at the Massachusetts Institute of Technology by Seymour Papert. Referred to as a "computer-based learning environment," it was originally designed as an educational tool for young children. It is not an acronym; it is derived from the Greek word for "word" or "thought."

loop A series of instructions or one instruction in a program that is repeated for a prescribed number of times, followed by a branch instruction that exits the program from the loop.

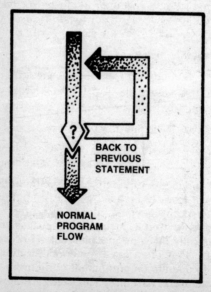

BACK TO PREVIOUS STATEMENT

NORMAL PROGRAM FLOW

loop

low-level language A set of machine-dependent instructions. Examples are assembly languages and machine languages. The instructions are, or are close to being, in a form that the computer can execute without complex translations. Usually, faster execution speeds or efficient memory storage are reasons for using low-level languages. Contrast with high-level languages.

A **LP** <u>L</u>ine <u>P</u>rinter (acronym).

A **lpm** <u>l</u>ines <u>p</u>er <u>m</u>inute (acronym).

A **lps** <u>l</u>ines <u>p</u>er <u>s</u>econd (acronym).

A **LSI** <u>L</u>arge-<u>Sc</u>ale <u>I</u>ntegration (acronym).

machine In industry vernacular, a word often used synonymously for a computer or processing unit.

machine code Machine language instructions.

machine dependent Capable of being used only on the machine for which it was originally designed.

machine-independent language A programming language that can be used on any computer that has the appropriate compiler or interpreter. Programs written in high-level languages are theoretically machine independent. However, in practice, they often need some modifications in order to operate on equipment of different manufacturers. Assembly languages are never machine independent; their instructions are

designed exclusively for a specific type of
processor.

machine language The language at its lowest level
(in binary form), into which data and programs must
ultimately be translated before the machine can
use it and execute any instructions.

00111110   01011000   11011011   00000011   11100110

---

machine language

macroassembler A special assembler that
recognizes key words in the assembly code and
expands them into their full instruction set. The
user defines the macro keywords and their
corresponding instruction set.

macroinstructions (1) A frequently used set of
predefined instructions designed to perform a
specific operation. The function is associated with
one code word that is defined by the user. Code
words (macros) are inserted within the main
program where needed. The code word references
the predefined macroinstruction set (body), which is
a separate machine language routine or assembly
routine. Using a macro, a user can define a
recurring task just once and then, when that task
is called for, the macro can be substituted. This will
shorten program length, but a special macroassembly
program is necessary to expand the macro into its
body and into machine code. The macro is a shared
resource in that its access is not restricted to one
program.

A macro differs from a subroutine in that when
a macroprogram goes through the translation
(assembly) process, the code for the macro keyword is
actually inserted into the program. Therefore,
when the program is executed, those "substituted
statements" are read sequentially, and there is no
transfer of control to any other area of memory. A

subroutine, on the other hand, uses a call
statement that is executed in order to transfer
control to a different area.

(2) In word processing, the macro can be a
word or phrase that is called up when a code word
is used. The code word is sometimes called a
"token."

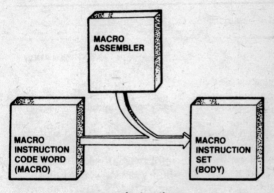

macro instructions

mag card Abbreviation for "magnetic card," a plastic,
flexible card about 3 inches × 7 inches with a
magnetized surface used for data storage.

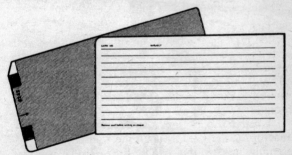

mag card

magnetic disk, layout A schematic representation of
common space allocations on a magnetic disk.

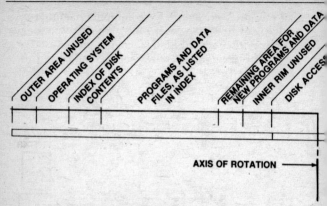

OUTER AREA UNUSED

OPERATING SYSTEM

INDEX OF DISK CONTENTS

PROGRAMS AND DATA FILES, AS LISTED IN INDEX

REMAINING AREA FOR NEW PROGRAMS AND DATA

INNER RIM UNUSED

DISK ACCESS

AXIS OF ROTATION ——→

magnetic disk, layout

magnetic tape A tape or ribbon coated with a magnetic material on which information may be placed in the form of magnetically polarized spots. See digital recording; cassette recording.

magnetic tape system High-capacity hardware storage, including tape drive and control circuitry. Because of the tape's serial access (in order to get to any one point, you must start at the beginning and cycle through), it is well suited for large batches of stored information that do not require frequent access or for applications where most of the records do not need to be accessed.

magnetic tape system

mail merge A procedure for combining names and
addresses from one record file with correspondence
from another record file for mailing purposes.
Also, the term for software that accomplishes this
task.

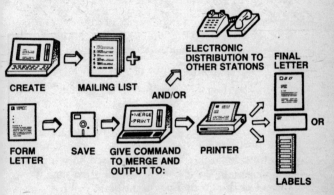

mail merge

main frame (1) A large computer in both size and
capacity. (2) The housing for computer circuit
boards. (3) The main portion of the computer,
containing the central processing unit (CPU),
memory, input/output, and power pack.

main memory Immediately accessible memory for
programs and data storage. It normally includes
ROM and RAM, but excludes mass storage
devices. Main memory is integral to the computer.
Also called internal memory.

management information system (MIS). Provides
business information helpful to managers,
including inventory, sales, payroll, and accounts
payable and receivable.

manipulation The act of changing or arranging data or
their format for ease of processing or to arrive at a
solution to a problem.

mantissa The significant digits of a number written

in scientific notation. For example, in the number 1.279×10^{12}, the mantissa is 1.279.

map A listing indicating where different elements of memory are laid out, such as the operating system, libraries, etc.

mapping (1) Transforming one set of information to another set. (2) Setting up the correspondence between one set of information and another set.

mark Indicates the presence of current, or binary 1.

mask (1) In integrated circuit (IC) technology, a template, usually etched on glass and used to define areas of the chip on the silicon wafer. Masks are used for the diffusion, oxidation, and metalizing steps in the process of manufacturing chips. (2) In computer logic, a pattern of bits used to selectively set, ignore, or clear bits within the word or bit pattern that is to be operated upon.

mass storage Large-capacity (megabytes, gigabytes) secondary storage systems. Typical mass storage devices are recording tape and magnetic disks. Also called external memory.

match A data processing operation used to compare items of data for identity. Sequences are matched against each other on the basis of a given key. A two-item match is represented by the schematic illustration:

Mattel A manufacturer of small computer systems and computer games.

MB MegaBytes (acronym).

media eraser An electromagnetic device that can completely erase stored data from any flexible magnetic media—tape, diskette, cassette, or data cartridge. See degausser.

mega Prefix meaning one million.

megabyte (MB or M-BYTE) 1,024 Kilobytes, or 1,024 × 1,024 bytes.

membrane keyboard A type of keyboard composed of a single sheet of semiflexible plastic material with a conductive rear surface. When flexed approximately 0.005 inch with slight finger pressure, contact results, and the signal is transmitted.

memory A temporary storage area for information (programs and data) in binary form.

memory, external See mass storage.

memory, internal See main memory.

memory management A method that utilizes both hardware and software techniques to control and allocate memory resources efficiently.

memory-mapped video A system in CRT high-resolution graphics displays in which each individual pixel position on the screen has a unique memory location or locations assigned to it. This is for storing data describing updated display attributes for that particular pixel, such as on/off, blinking, color, etc.

memory-mapped I/O A technique in which addresses placed in peripheral devices "appear" to the processor as memory locations. The processor can send data to, or receive data from, the peripherals using the same instructions it uses to

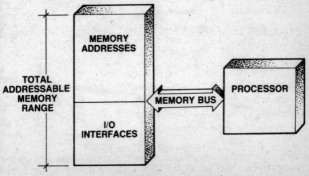

memory-mapped I/O

access memory. The advantage is that existing
processor instructions can serve this dual purpose.
The disadvantage is that this procedure diminishes
the range of memory locations used for programs
and data.

memory mapping A listing of memory addresses
showing how the system memory is allocated among
various devices or programs.

memory protect A feature designed to prevent
accidental modification of the operating systems.
It separates the operating system from the user
programs. This hardware protection of certain
areas of memory inhibits unauthorized reading from,
or writing to, designated areas.

menu A program-generated list of options, usually
presented on the display screen, to which the user
can refer and from which the user can select in
order to execute desired procedures.

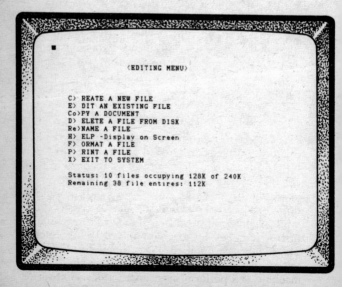

```
                    ⟨EDITING MENU⟩


          C⟩ REATE A NEW FILE
          E⟩ DIT AN EXISTING FILE
          Co⟩PY A DOCUMENT
          D⟩ ELETE A FILE FROM DISK
          Re⟩NAME A FILE
          H⟩ ELP -Display on Screen
          F⟩ ORMAT A FILE
          P⟩ RINT A FILE
          X⟩ EXIT TO SYSTEM

          Status: 10 files occupying 128K of 240K
          Remaining 38 file entires: 112K
```

menu

merge The combination of records from two or more ordered input files into a single, consecutively ordered output file.

A **MHz** <u>M</u>ega<u>H</u>ertz (acronym).

micro From the Greek letter mu, meaning very small.

microcomputer, 8-bit A computer system utilizing a central processing unit that has 8-bit word size. See microcomputer architecture.

microcomputer, 8/16 bit A system that uses a processor with a 16-bit word size, but which multiplexes data across an external 8-line data bus. The larger word size increases the amount of memory that can be addressed and enables more precise and complex instruction sets. See microcomputer architecture.

microcomputer, 16-bit A computer utilizing a central processing unit (CPU) that has 16-bit word size. See microcomputer architecture.

microcomputer, 16/32 bit A system that uses a 32-bit processor, but which multiplexes data across an external 16-line data bus. The larger word size provides for more precision of calculation and complexity of instructions. The larger data bus enables faster transfer of data to and from storage. See microcomputer architecture.

microcomputer architecture The architecture of a microcomputer is designated in terms of bits—8 bit, 16 bit, 32 bit, etc.—indicating the size of the "chunk" of data that can be handled in one execution (read, write, move, etc.) and the number of memory cells in which data can be stored. An 8-bit machine moves 8 bits of data in a machine instruction; a 16-bit machine moves 16 bits, etc. The higher the number of bits defined in the microcomputer architecture, the faster the machine will perform most instructions. Software created on an 8-bit machine usually will not run on a 16-bit machine. See microcomputer, 8 bit; microcomputer, 8/16 bit; microcomputer, 16 bit; microcomputer, 16/32 bit; word size.

microcomputer system A complete small system, including the central processing unit (CPU), input/output interfaces and devices, memory and power supply, alphanumerical keyboard, CRT display, and mass-memory device. Generally smaller than a minicomputer in physical size, word size, memory size, and other factors, they are single-user systems referred to as "personal" computers and "desktop" computers. There is a range of storage capacities available, and this capacity is partially dependent on word size (8-bit, 16-bit, or 32-bit).

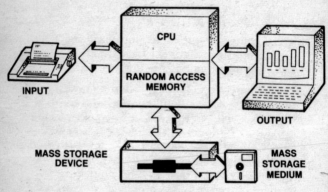

microcomputer system

microfloppy A floppy disk characterized by a 3-inch-

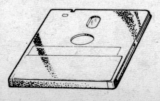

microfloppy disk

or 3.5-inch-square disk jacket. Contrast with
minifloppy (5.25 inch) or floppy (8 inch).

microinstructions A simple instruction representing
one step in a process; e.g., an assembly instruction
might consist of microinstructions such as: move
data in register to accumulator; move contents of a
memory location to the data bus; etc. These types
of instructions are internal to the specific computer.

microprocessor A central processing unit consisting
of an arithmetic logical unit (ALU) and a control unit
(CU) organized on one or more chips by means of
large-scale integration (LSI) technology. A
microprocessor is used as the central processing
unit (CPU) of a microcomputer system and is often
referred to as the microprocessor unit. It
accomplishes its results by moving data around or
by performing calculations.

microprocessor, 8-bit A microprocessor that has
8-bit registers and manipulates data that are in the
form of 8-bit words.

microprocessor, 16-bit A microprocessor that has a
16-bit word size. The ability to handle words that
are twice as big (compared to the standard 8-bit
word size) means that it can process twice as
much data at a time. It also offers greater speed and
precision (accurate to a greater number of
significant figures) than an 8-bit processor.
Sixteen-bit processors also have more powerful
and complex instruction sets.

microprocessor unit (MPU). See microprocessor.

microprogram A sequence written in microinstructions
and stored in the control unit of the microprocessor
unit. When executed, it will perform the function
of various microinstructions. The microprogram
references the control unit directly; it is not
accessible to the user.

microworld A well-defined but limited learning
environment in which interesting happenings occur

and important ideas are offered. A microworld can have other microworlds within.

minicomputer A faster, larger, more expensive computer than the micro. However, the dividing line between minicomputers and microcomputers is becoming less distinct. The term *mini* used to refer to a 16-bit machine, while a *micro* referred to an 8-bit machine. Today, there are 16-bit microcomputers and 32-bit minicomputers.

minifloppy A floppy-disk size designation characterized by its 5.25-inch-square (13.3 cm) protective jacket. Also diskette.

A MIS Management Information System (acronym).

mnemonic An easily remembered word chosen to represent another word, phrase, or concept that is more difficult to remember.

modem modulator-demodulator (acronym). A device that connects peripherals and that converts and reconverts digital signals from a computer into tone variations (in serial form) for transmission over standard telephone communication lines. See acoustic coupler; modem communication; modem, direct connect.

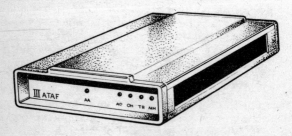

modem

modem bypass A special cable that allows a local device to be connected directly to a modem communication port. It is used when modem communication is not necessary but operation of the local device is. For example, the user may not wish to disconnect the modem but might have need of another terminal. The terminal could be attached to the bypass and then disconnected for later use of the modem.

modem communication The process of using modems for communication between computers or between computers and peripherals. For example, data flow from a computer through a modem, where digital signals are converted to audio signals, then across telephone lines to another modem that reconverts the audio information into digital signals that can be used by the receiving device or terminal.

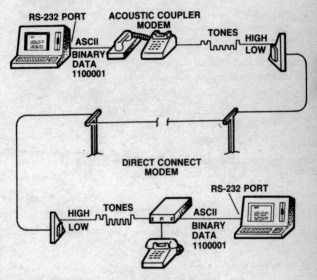

modem communications

modem, direct connect A type of modem that is connected electrically (by means of a plug) to the telephone system and eliminates the need for an acoustic coupler connection or telephone instrument.

TO POWER SUPPLY

modem, direct connect

module A building block that can be used to create a larger whole. In software, a subroutine can be considered a module; in hardware, any device that can be combined with others to create a larger system.

monitor See video monitor.

B MOS Metal Oxide Semiconductor (acronym). The high-density integrated circuit technology used for most large-scale integration (LSI) devices, including microprocessors.

most significant bit The bit in the left-most position of a binary word. See least significant bit; significant figures.

ONE BINARY WORD

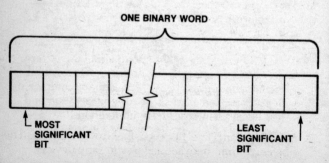

MOST
SIGNIFICANT
BIT

LEAST
SIGNIFICANT
BIT

most significant bit

mother board A main hardware board within the system. It is equipped with female connectors into which all the circuit boards are plugged. Also called a "backplane."

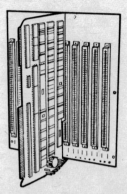

mother board (with CPU board attached)

Motorola Manufacturers of electronic equipment, including the Motorola 6800, 6809, and M68000 microprocessors.

mouse A cursor positioning device, manipulated by hand, that moves the screen cursor in the same direction as the movement created when the mouse is rolled on any flat surface. See track ball.

A **MPU** Micro Processor Unit (acronym). See microprocessor.

A **ms** millisecond. One thousandth of a second.

A **MSI** Medium Scale Integration (acronym). A term that describes the amount, or density, of integrated circuitry in a given area. MSI is more complex or densely packed than small-scale integration and less dense than large-scale integration.

A **MTBF** Mean Time Between Failures (acronym). The average time between failures for any device.

multiplexing The ability for two or more signals to

share the same line but to remain independent of and distinct from each other.

multiplexor A device which combines two or more signals into one output signal and also has the capability to separate component signals from the one incoming signal.

multiprecision arithmetic Using more than one word to define the numbers in a computation; the larger word size permits greater accuracy.

multiprocessing Multiple processors being used in one system for separate functions. The functions may be unique or overlapping, depending on the arrangement.

multitasking A mode of computer operation in which the concurrent execution of two or more programs occurs under one operating system. Routines, memory space, and disk files that are held in common (accessible to all) may be used. The operations will appear to be simultaneous but will be truly simultaneous only in a multiprocessor system.

multiuser system A system in which computers, terminals, and other peripherals are shared in any one of several arrangements.

multiviewports A display that is able simultaneously to generate two or more viewing screens that are adjacent but independent. See split screen.

multiviewports

N

NAND A Boolean operative which produces a true (1) output only if all inputs are not equal.

nanosecond One billionth of a second (10^{-9}).

native compiler A compiler that produces code usable only for a particular processor or brand of equipment.

N-channel MOS (NMOS). The metal oxide semiconductor technology for large-scale integration (LSI) devices developed after PMOS. It has a higher speed but lower density than PMOS.

NE A notation for NOT EQUAL TO used with logical programming statements. Other notations of inequality are LT (less than), or GT (greater than).

NEC Nippon Electric Co. Information Systems Inc., manufacturers of computer systems and printers.

negative-true logic A system of logic where a high voltage represents the bit value 0 and a low voltage represents the bit value 1. This is the reverse of traditional logical representation.

nesting A programming technique that involves hierarchical levels of instructions, usually in subroutines, that are called in a specific order. It may be thought of as instruction loops within other instruction loops. See loop.

network A series of interconnected computers,

peripherals, and/or terminals communicating with each other.

network, bus A popular local-area network (LAN) configuration that utilizes a long length of cable (often coaxial) running near each station. Each station may exist on individual short branch segments connected to the common cable. A node, or controller, connects the station to the cable, monitors the network traffic, and pulls off the communications addressed to the node. The signal passes in front of each station and can run in two directions. One advantage to a bus network is that if one access node fails, it usually does not bring down the entire system. It also is relatively easy to add stations to the network. Ethernet™ employs this form of interconnection.

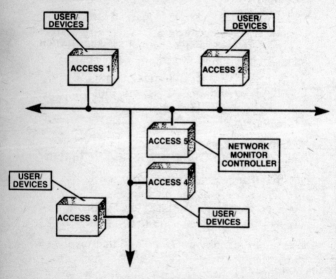

network, bus

network, data communications A service for distribution of information to subscribers, often throughout the country. Data from local sources are compressed into "packets" and sent in a continuous stream from point to point. At the destination, the data are routed over local lines to receiving terminals.

network, local-area (LAN). A system allowing several concentrations of computers and terminals within a local area to share resources such as peripherals, software, or data. This encourages low-cost, computer-based work stations throughout an office or campus, all of which have access to expensive peripherals such as hard-disk drives, printers, or data bases without the cost of equipment duplication. In addition, enhanced communication between work stations avoids repetition of work. Various configurations of networks are available, as well as gateways capable of connecting several networks to each other.

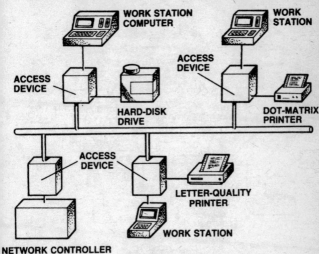

network, local-area

network, local-area, general-purpose A local-area network system that links a large community of different terminals, peripherals, and computers and is capable of supporting a wide range of data transmission speeds.

network, local-area, single-purpose A network system devoted to one application; the network interconnects computers and work stations of one manufacturer.

network, ring A local-area network arrangement in which signals pass through the nodes instead of in front of them, as in a bus network. The stations form a ring, often using coaxial cable. Each station connects to the cable via a controller that examines the messages on the network. If the message is for the station, the controller holds it for processing; if the message is for another station, the controller retransmits the message to the next station. Failure of one node can jeopardize the whole ring.

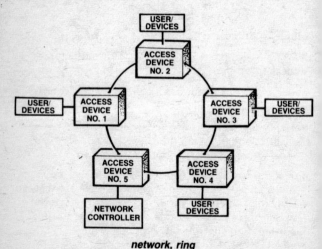

network, ring

network, star A local-area network in which individual stations branch from a central control node. Messages from one station to another are first routed to a central controller. The advantage is that Private Automatic Branch Exchanges (PABXs) are organized as star networks, which enables some companies to utilize their existing PABX wiring. However, if the central control node fails, the entire system shuts down. See PABX.

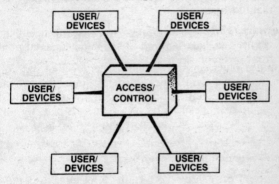

network, star

nibble Four bits or half a byte.

NMOS <u>N</u>-channel <u>M</u>etal <u>Ox</u>ide <u>S</u>emiconductor (acronym).

node A junction point of a diagram, or the control points in a network.

noise In a circuit, a random signal or other disturbance that may interfere with the flow of meaningful signals or information.

nonprint character A control character that can invoke a special function, but which has no printed symbol. Depending on the software, the symbol may or may not be visible on the screen during editing. See control character.

nonvolatile memory Memory that retains its contents when power is shut off.

NOR A Boolean operative whose definition is that the output is 1 (true) only when neither of the inputs are 1 (true).

NOT The logical negation operator. It changes every 1 to 0 and every 0 to 1 in a collection of binary data. See Boolean Algebra.

null An absence of information used as a positive confirmation of no information, as opposed to a 0 or a blank.

null cycle The time required to cycle through the entire program without introducing new data.

null instruction A program instruction that has no functional significance during program execution, but which may satisfy a structural requirement such as breaking a program into segments or reserving memory space for an instruction to be inserted later.

null modem See modem bypass.

number crunching Performing a lot of arithmetic functions—usually repetitive or complex—as opposed to moving data in the computer system.

number system, base Number systems vary principally by their base. The choice of the base can be advantageous for a particular application. The base is indicated in subscript notation. For example,

HEXADECIMAL	DECIMAL	OCTAL	BINARY
0	0	0	0000
1	1	1	0001
2	2	2	0010
3	3	3	0011
4	4	4	0100
5	5	5	0101
6	6	6	0110
7	7	7	0111
8	8	10	1000
9	9	11	1001
A	10	12	1010
B	11	13	1011
C	12	14	1100
D	13	15	1101
E	14	16	1110
F	15	17	1111
10	16	20	10000

number systems

10001_2, $6F_{16}$, 850_{10}. The accompanying chart illustrates a few number systems used in association with computers. See base.

numerical analysis Use of computing systems to solve mathematical problems; e.g., equations and matrix manipulation in contrast to record keeping.

numerical keypad A set of auxiliary keys at the right of the standard alphanumerical keyboard, with numbers for use in efficient input of numerical data. It is a convenient auxiliary to the alphanumeric keyboard. See keypad.

numerical processor chip A processor specifically designed to handle high-precision arithmetic and scientific function evaluation.

object program Once a program has been translated to machine language by a compiler or assembler, the resultant machine language instructions are referred to as the object program. Contrast with source program.

A OCR Optical Character Recognition (acronym).

octal A number system with base 8.

A OEM Original Equipment Manufacturer (acronym). A company that either packages different components, or components and software, for the purpose of selling them to an end user for a specific function. See turnkey.

off-line When the operation of equipment or

devices is not under the control of the central processing unit.

Okidata Manufacturer of a popular line of printers.

one-chip computer Describes the case when all the elements of a computer—RAM, ROM, CPU and input/output interfaces—are implemented on a single chip.

on-line The situation in which the operation and control of the system and its peripheral equipment are working under control of the central processing unit.

B OPCODE OPerating CODE (acronym).

operand An item, quantity, or memory location upon which a mathematical or logical operation is performed.

operating system (OS). The control system under which all other software functions. Software that runs the system and performs functions necessary to control system operations. Input/output, debugging, storage assignment tasks, compiling, and reporting system status are some operating system tasks. Operating systems usually are delivered by the vendor with the hardware.

operation (1) The action specified by one computer instruction. (2) Performing arithmetic, logical, or manipulative actions on data.

operation code The command component of a computer instruction, specifying the actual operation to be performed; e.g., ADD (add), MUL (multiply), etc. Commands that are not operation codes will typically be operands and may specify registers, addresses, data, etc.

operator (1) A logical or mathematical symbol or character that represents a process to be performed on an operand such as " + ," " − ," AND, OR, etc. (2) A person or machine (such as a robot) that operates a machine.

optical character recognition (OCR). A process by which photosensitive devices are able to identify printed graphic characters. As the machine recognizes the characters, equivalent codes are automatically entered into the computer's memory for storage and later recall. Also automatic document entry (ADE). See character recognition.

optical wand See bar-code reader.

OR A Boolean operative whose definition is that the output is 1 (true) only if at least one of the inputs is 1 (true). This is used to compare logically two or more states.

ordering The process of arranging groups of characters by sorting and sequencing them in some arbitrary manner; e.g., ascending or descending.

A **OS** Operating System (acronym).

output table The bed, or flat surface, of a plotter.

overflow A condition caused by an arithmetic operation that generates a number that is too big for either the hardware or software word-size limitations of the machine.

overlay A technique for bringing routines into main memory from some other form of storage during processing so that several routines will occupy the same storage locations at different times. Overlay is used when the total storage requirement for instructions exceeds the available main storage.

overprint To print over a previously printed character

```
!--------------------------------------------------!
!                                                  !
!   THIS IS AN EXAMPLE OF OVERPRINTING TO CREATE   !
!                                                  !
!   BOLD FACE for emphasis                         !
!                                                  !
!     DOUBLE STRIKE for emphasis but not as heavy as bold face !
!                                                  !
!     OVERPRINTING for various effects for a character !
!                                                  !
!   or an entire line to indicate a strikeout;     !
!                                                  !
!--------------------------------------------------!
```

overprinting

or characters in order to emphasize or improve the type. Also overstrike.

A PABX Private Automatic Branch eXchange (acronym).

packet A short, fixed-length block of data used for transmission. Each packet contains bits for control information such as address, routing, security, error control, etc., as well as data. See packet switching network.

packet switching network A network of devices that communicate by means of packets of information. Each device requires software to identify which packets to keep and which to send on.

packing density The number of units of information contained within a given linear dimension; e.g., one type of tape drive has a packing density of 1,600 bits per inch (bpi).

paddle A cursor control device used for computer games.

paddles

page (1) A logical fixed-length block of data or a program subdivision treated as an entity in storage. It can be shuffled back and forth from main memory to secondary memory in order to optimize main memory space. (2) A segment of memory organized for a particular purpose. (3) To call into memory, or send to secondary storage, a page of data. (4) A screenful of information on a CRT screen. See scrolling.

paper feed The method by which paper is pulled through a printer. See friction feed; tractor feed.

paper tape An old but reliable storage medium by which data are stored as punched-hole sequences on a paper tape. The technique is slow but inexpensive.

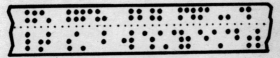

paper tape

parallel processing A computer operation during which two programs run concurrently, using more than one central processing unit.

parallel storage Storage in which all elements of a word are handled at the same time.

parallel transmission Transfer of data so that all bits

1	⟶	⊓ 1
0	⟶	— 2
1	⟶	⊓ 1
1	⟶	⊓ 1
1	⟶	⊓ 1
0	⟶	— 2
0	⟶	— 2
1	⟶	⊓ 1

1 = VOLTAGE PRESENT
2 = NO CURRENT

parallel transmission

are transmitted simultaneously, each one over a separate path. Parallel transmission requires more equipment than serial transmission but is faster. Parallel transmission cannot use standard RS-232 parts for communication.

parameter (1) A variable whose value is set in the main program and passed along to a subroutine, and vice versa. (2) A definable characteristic, or one of a set, whose value determines the values and limitations of a system.

parity check An error-detection technique for checking the accuracy of computer words after transmission. One extra parity bit is included with each character (byte). In an "even" parity convention, the parity bit is set to 0 only if the sum of digits in the original word is an even number. The reverse holds in an "odd" convention. If a single bit changes state because a

PARITY BIT

1 1 0 0 1 1 0 1 NUMBER OF 1 BITS = 5

0 1 1 0 0 1 0 0 NUMBER OF 1 BITS = 3

A. ODD PARITY

PARITY BIT

0 1 0 1 0 1 0 1 NUMBER OF 1 BITS = 4

1 0 1 1 0 1 1 1 NUMBER OF 1 BITS = 6

B. EVEN PARITY

parity

hardware malfunction has occurred, the parity check will detect an inconsistency.

partial RAM A RAM in which some bits do not function. In some of the newer 64K chips, as many as half of the bit locations turn out to be unusable.

Pascal A high-level programming language known for features that promote structured programming, block structure, and data types. Invented by Niklaus Wirth but named for the seventeenth-century French mathematician and philosopher Blaise Pascal. See structured programming.

patch A section of code used to correct or alter a program. It is inserted into a program in an ad hoc manner after the program has been completed. It will not be directly inserted into the program until the program is rewritten.

pattern recognition The recognition and identification by a computer of shapes, forms, signals, sequences, and configurations. See character recognition.

A **PC** _P_rinted _C_ircuit (acronym).

A **PC** _P_ersonal _C_omputer (acronym).

A **PCI/O** _P_rogram _C_ontrolled _I_nput/_O_utput (acronym).

P-code A method of translating a source code to an intermediate code, called P-code, by means of a compiler, then using a special P-code interpreter on a host machine to obtain executable object code. The advantage of this approach is portability; each host machine needs only its own P-code interpreter

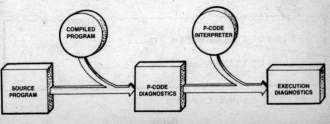

P-code

and not a separate compiler. The compiler module is standard for all machines. The disadvantage is that the execution is slower than occurs with one-step translation to object code. Many versions of Pascal use P-code.

peek A statement in the BASIC Programming Language that displays the contents of a particular memory location in decimal form.

performance degradation (1) Any situation in which the performance of the system is not optimal; for example, when two or more programs are competing for necessary resources. (2) Hardware failure of a component.

peripheral A device, usually for input/output, such as storage or printing, connected to a computer and under its control to some degree. Examples include, but are not limited to: printers, card readers, tape drives, disk drives, terminals.

peripheral processor See input/output processor.

peripheral slots Holding slots built into the housing of some microprocessor units so that cards can be added in order to increase capabilities without hardware modification.

perpendicular recording A recording technology that replaces traditional longitudinal, or end-to-end,

LONGITUDINAL

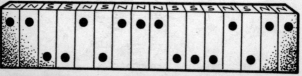

PERPENDICULAR

perpendicular record

organization of magnets along the recording track with vertically oriented magnets in order to increase potential recording capacity.

personal computer A moderately priced, general-use computer designed principally for a single user in a home or small-office environment.

B PERT <u>P</u>rogram <u>E</u>valuation and <u>R</u>eview <u>T</u>echniques (acronym). A system from which the critical path method was derived and which is very similar. See critical-path method.

phoneme One member of the set of the smallest components of speech, which distinguishes individual utterances from each other in a language.

phonetic system A system that uses a data base of voice information (phonemes) to produce sounds that emulate speech.

phosphor dots The minute particles of phosphor on a CRT picture tube used to create the image. On a color picture tube, combinations of red, blue, and green phosphor dots are organized in a pattern of dot triads.

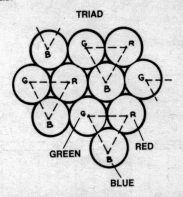

phosphor dots

physical record A unit of information contained within a specific, addressable location on a storage medium, such as a magnetic disk or tape, and which is stored all in one unit instead of scattered as in a logical record.

A PIC Priority Intercept Controller (acronym). A special chip utilized to manage several external interrupts. It decides priority in a situation of simultaneous interrupts and in some cases interrupts servicing of devices that have low priority in favor of devices that have higher priority. See priority interrupt.

picosecond 10^{-12} or one trillionth of a second.

picture element See pixel.

piezoelectric A property of some crystals, resulting in mechanical stress when subjected to voltages, or producing voltage when subjected to mechanical stress.

pin-compatible Devices that use the same conventions with regard to accepting certain electronic signals. Each pin receives only a specific signal.

pin feed The pin mechanism of a printer, which guides the punched holes of fan-fold paper through the sprocket. Also tractor feed, sprocket feed.

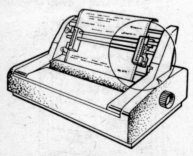

pin feed

pipelining The starting execution of one computer instruction before a previous instruction is completely executed.

A PIT <u>P</u>rogrammable <u>I</u>nterval <u>T</u>imer (acronym).

pixel Abbreviation for picture element. The basic rectangular element that, in combinations, forms the images on the video screen.

platen The backing that a print element strikes against to make character imprints.

PLATO A computer-based educational system that consists of a large, high-speed central computer that can service up to 1,000 terminals in a time-share mode. It is geared to individual instruction consisting of interactive lessons, with the student entering responses via the keyboard or touching answers displayed on the screen. The system is currently being implemented for use with microprocessors.

A PL/1 <u>P</u>rogramming <u>L</u>anguage <u>1</u> (acronym). A high-level language developed in the mid-1960s that combines features useful for both scientific and data processing applications.

A PL/M <u>P</u>rogramming <u>L</u>anguage for <u>M</u>icroprocessors (acronym). Derived from PL/1 but for use on microprocessors.

plotter A device for producing hard copy of graphic

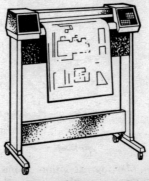

plotter

images by controlling pens or other drawing media. A plotter addresses points related to X and Y coordinate axes in a (seemingly) random fashion, as compared to a printer that produces successive lines and columns of type. See flatbed plotter.

plug-compatible The ability to interchange one device for another, usually without modifying the hardware or the software.

C **PMOS** <u>P</u>-channel <u>M</u>etal <u>O</u>xide <u>S</u>emiconductor (acronym). A relatively old MOS technology for large-scale integration (LSI) devices. It is characterized by high circuitry density but slow microprocessor speed when compared to NMOS.

pointer An address used to locate some data at a specific location in memory. This item of data contains an address (points to a memory location) of another item of data.

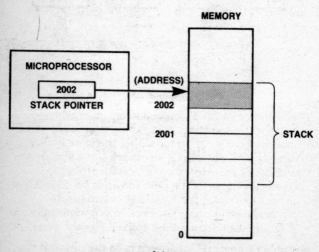

pointer

poke A statement used in BASIC programming language to place data directly into a specified memory location.

Polish notation An arbitrary way to state mathematical relationships in order to avoid parentheses. For example, $(A + B) \times (C + D)$ might be written as $A\,B + C\,D + \times$, which means: get A and B, then add; get C and D, then add; then multiply. This offers advantages in hardware and software design.

polling A technique to identify which input/output device among several is trying to get the processor's attention so it can be serviced.

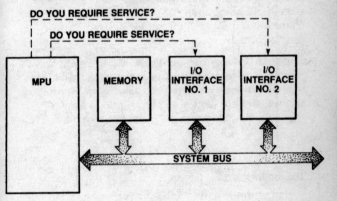

DO YOU REQUIRE SERVICE?

DO YOU REQUIRE SERVICE?

| MPU | MEMORY | I/O INTERFACE NO. 1 | I/O INTERFACE NO. 2 |

SYSTEM BUS

polling

port An input/output connection for interfacing peripherals and computers. The port consists of a male or female connector with a specific number of pins; each pin carries an agreed-upon signal. A number of standards have evolved for pin connectors. One of the best known is RS-232. All of the devices using the RS-232 standard can be physically connected; however, appropriate software is required to decode the received signal.

portable computer Usually refers to the physical size of certain computers that may be conveniently hand carried and are about the same dimensions as a small briefcase. Compare with handheld, briefcase, and desktop computer.

portable computer

portability The ability of a program to be used on more than one system. Theoretically, programs written in high-level languages are portable. In reality, variations between manufacturers' systems require some degree of modification of most programs that are used on different systems. Only subsets of a language are, therefore, truly portable.

positive true logic A logic system where a lower voltage represents a bit value of 0 and a higher voltage represents a bit value of 1.

power supply The unit, usually within the computer housing, that converts the alternating current (AC)

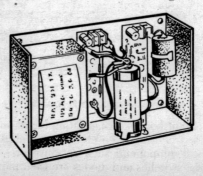

power supply

line voltage from the wall outlet to the direct current (DC) required by individual electrical components.

powerful (1) Software is considered powerful if it is efficient and it provides a wide range of options. In user software, it refers to the user's ability to put these options into action without too much effort. In system software, it denotes the ability to generate complex commands with a minimum of instructions. (2) Hardware is considered powerful if it is faster, larger, and more versatile than comparable machines.

precision The "exactness" or accuracy associated with a number. For example, 5.1234 has 5 digits of precision; if it were to have 3 digits, it would be rounded off to 5.12.

preprocessor A program used in emulation to convert data from one format, that of the system being emulated, into the format that will be accepted by the emulator.

pressure-sensitive keyboard See membrane keyboard.

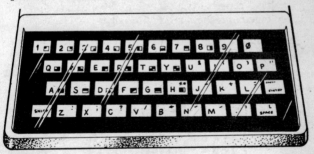

pressure-sensitive keyboard

printed circuit board An insulating board onto which a circuit has been etched or printed. Electrical components such as transistors, resistors, switches and diodes are then mounted on the board. Same as printed circuit card.

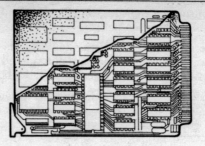

printed circuit board

printer An output device for producing hard copy. See dot-matrix printer; letter-quality printer.

printer, dual-mode A dot-matrix printer that produces characters on paper at one rate for near-letter-quality printing for word processing (average 100 cps) and at a faster rate (average 160 cps) for draft-quality results in data processing.

printout Hard copy produced by a printer.

priority interrupt A system of interrupt in which devices of a higher priority may obtain servicing by the central processing unit (CPU) before lower-priority devices.

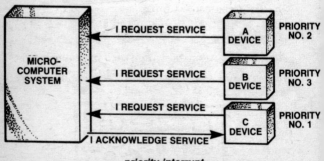

priority interrupt

private automatic branch exchange (PABX). A private automatic telephone switching system that controls the transmission of calls to and from the public telephone network.

processor bound A situation in which the limits of the speed of a computation are determined by the capabilities of the processor. See I/O bound.

program A sequence of instructions given to the computer to perform specific functions or tasks. Programs are also referred to as "software." See software; applications software.

program chaining A technique for allowing programs to be run that are larger than main memory by sequential loading and executing of successive modules of that program.

program counter A register in the control unit of the CPU that contains the address of the next instruction to be fetched from memory. The program counter is automatically incremented after each instruction is fetched.

programmable communications interface An interface board used for communications control in which major features, such as baud rate, are programmable rather than being preset (hard wired).

Programmable Read-Only Memory (PROM) Similar to ROM but can be programmed once by the user. A special PROM programmer is used to write in the new program. See EPROM.

programmer A person who writes programs.

programmer's template A pattern guide on which

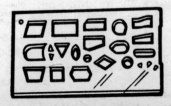

programmer's template

there are flowchart, logical and other symbols used in programming.

B PROM Programmable ROM (acronym).

prompt A symbol generated on an input/output terminal; its purpose is to make the user either aware of the necessity of further input or of the location of an input.

proof-copy mode The ability of a printer to make a proof copy with notations, highlighting, or symbols to mark revisions.

proportional spacing The ability of a printer to allocate spaces in tiny increments in order to compensate for the varying widths of the characters. Although more complex routines are necessary, the output appears more pleasing than output in which characters are given equal space regardless of width. This is essential to production of completely justified copy.

proprietary software Programs written by and/or controlled by an owner who has legal rights and titles. Copy and/or disclosure of program contents cannot be made by another party without prior agreement between owner and second party. Usually protected by copyright.

prosthetic Sometimes used to refer to the computer's use as a versatile tool that provides access to a large variety of inaccessible spaces and activities.

protected field (1) An area on the CRT screen containing data that cannot be altered by an operator until it is freed by a special command. (2) An area of memory that cannot be altered by a user program.

protocol A set of conventions governing the transfer or exchange of information between two systems or devices. For example, a CPU cannot talk to a printer until there is an agreement as to which circuits will carry signaling (operating) information and which circuits will carry data. In addition, there must be agreement as to which bit configuration will trigger a specific event, such as a printer line feed. These conventions are defined as recognized sets of standards called protocols.

public-domain software Software that is not copyrighted and that can be freely exchanged and copied.

pulse A significant and sudden change, which is of short duration, in the intensity of an electrical variable such as voltage.

punch card A standardized stiff paper card used for storing information via strategically punched holes. The card can be handled mechanically and machine processed; the punched holes are sensed electrically by metal fingers or photoelectrically by photo cells.

punch card

push-down list A list organization in which the last (newest) item added becomes the first in the list and is the first to be retrieved. All other items are pushed back (down) one from the previously existing order.

push-down stack A set of computer registers or memory locations that uses the push-down list concept. (See preceding entry.)

push-up list The organization of a list in which the last item stored is entered at the end of the list, retaining the existing order of the items on the list.

push-up storage A method of storing data that retrieves the items in the same order in which they were entered; that is, the oldest piece of data is the first to be retrieved.

quad Involving four elements.

quad capacity A floppy disk with double-density, double-sided recording characteristics in order to achieve more storage per disk.

query language A user friendly set of commands that allow a user to access information from a data base. See user friendly.

queue A line of items waiting for service or processing, such as data to be processed by a central processing unit, or terminals waiting for access to a system. Requests for service are usually queued so as to be handled in some designated order.

queuing theory A form of probability theory useful in studying delays or lineups at service points. Can be applied to the movement of bits of information, auto assembly lines, pedestrian traffic circulation, etc.

QWERTY keyboard The name used for the standard typewriter keyboard layout and containing those six letters in one row in that arrangement.

This is the keyboard layout found in microcomputer terminals. See Dvorak keyboard.

QWERTY keyboard

A R Read (acronym).

A R/W <u>R</u>ead/<u>W</u>rite memory (acronym).

Radio Shack A distributor of electronic equipment, hardware, and software, including the TRS-80 computers and TRSDOS operating system. All are products of Tandy Corporation.

radix The base of a number system. For example, the binary system radix is 2; the decimal system radix is 10; octal is 8, etc. See base.

B RAM <u>R</u>andom <u>A</u>ccess <u>M</u>emory (acronym).

random access The process of obtaining data from or placing data into a storage location in which access is not restricted by sequential search of the data. The order of retrieval is independent of the order of storage.

random-access memory (RAM). This memory storage area for programs and data is immediately accessible to and directly addressable by the central processing unit (CPU). Data can be read from or written into RAM memory location, and the location can be reached via random access. Normally, all user programs are in RAM. RAM differs from ROM (read-only memory) in that RAM can be altered and programs written in, while in ROM, no alteration is possible. Another major difference is that information in RAM is not retained when the power is turned off, but information does remain in ROM after the electricity has been shut off.

raster The predetermined pattern of horizontal lines on the viewing screen of a cathode ray tube. The lines are scanned by an electron beam and are spaced to aid uniform area coverage. See raster scan.

raster scan (CRT display). A display technology in which an image is built from phosphor dots of varying intensity, illuminated by the focus of an electron beam. Since the luminescent quality of the phosphor does not last long, continued regeneration by the electron beam is needed to maintain the image. This is the type of system used for most black and white, and color, television sets, as well as many computer displays. See cathode ray tube; interlaced field; phosphor dots; raster.

raw data Data before they have been processed, and which may not be in a form comprehensible to the machine.

read To receive data from a device and to interpret them in preparation for processing.

read-only memory (ROM). A memory circuit written during manufacture that cannot be altered by a user, program, or other means.

read/write head An electromagnetic device used to read from or write to a magnetic storage medium such as a disk or tape. See digital recording.

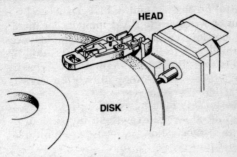

read/write head

read/write memory See random-access memory.

real time Processing that occurs simultaneously with some physical event, with the purpose of controlling or affecting that event without causing delay. The information must be processed right away, or at an exact moment, or it will be lost or useless.

record A group of related fields of information treated as a unit for organizational purposes. A record may be one of many within a file. Each record may be similar in form and content; e.g., information about a customer. The way a user sees a record is always in its logical (assembled) form regardless of its actual location.

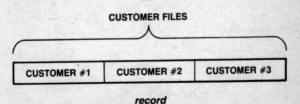

record

recursive routine or procedure A routine or procedure that calls itself, or that calls a different

procedure or routine, which, in turn, calls the
first one again. This type of processing develops a
set of levels and is related to tree structures. See
tree structure.

reduction, data Taking raw (unprocessed) data and
converting them into useful, understandable data.

redundancy (1) Use of several devices that all
perform the same function in order to increase that
function's reliability or accuracy. (2) When
transmitting information, the portion that can be
permitted to be lost without impairment or loss of
crucial information. (3) Those areas or devices that
overlap or are repetitious.

redundant recording A cassette tape recording
method where each piece of information is stored
twice on the tape as insurance against information
loss in the event of damage to any portion of the
tape.

reel-to-reel A type of ribbon or tape feed used on
some printers.

refresh The continuing process of regenerating a
signal over and over again in a situation where it
decays or fades when left idle. The cells in a
dynamic memory chip and the phosphor-illuminated
image on a CRT screen are examples.

registers Temporary storage or processing areas
designed for fast access by the microprocessor unit
(MPU). They are usually internal to the MPU and
directly addressable to it (more quickly than main
memory).

regression analysis Found in statistical analysis, a
means of determining rate of change.

relocatable program A module of an object program
or routine that does not have a fixed address and
that is structured so that it can be moved and
executed from any location in main memory
without loss of efficiency.

repeat counter A software counter that records the number of times an event takes place in a program for later comparison.

repeat key (1) A key that can be held down so that it repeatedly makes contact without need for additional depression. (2) A key that is pressed at the same time as another key in order to make the second key repeat for the duration of the time that the repeat key is depressed. For example, it can be used in combination with the cursor movement keys in order to move rapidly across the screen.

repeatability The ability of a device to minimize variation each time it performs a repetitive operation that is based on a constant input signal. It is often expressed as a percentage of error.

report generation Production of a report as output, requiring only the specification of the arrangement and content desired, and designating existing data as input.

report generator A program that generates a report using designated specifications and existing data.

A **RES** **RES**et signal (acronym).

residual value The value of a piece of equipment at the end of a lease term.

retrofit Updating of or adding to an existing system in order to improve it or to accommodate a change.

return (1) An instruction used at the termination of a subroutine causing control to return to the main program. (2) See carriage return.

reverse video A cathode ray tube (CRT) display technique that shows dark characters against a light background for emphasis.

REVERSE NORMAL

reverse video

rewrite The process of putting out information to memory or a storage device.

A RF <u>R</u>adio <u>F</u>requency (acronym).

RF modulator (Radio Frequency modulator). A device that adapts a computer output signal so that it can be used with a standard television display. The RF modulator encodes the composite video output from the computer into a radio frequency signal for display on the television set.

A RGB monitor <u>R</u>ed, <u>G</u>reen, <u>B</u>lue Monitor (acronym). A type of color monitor with separate inputs for red, green, and blue; the type required for high-resolution color images. The red, green, and blue signals must be sent separately.

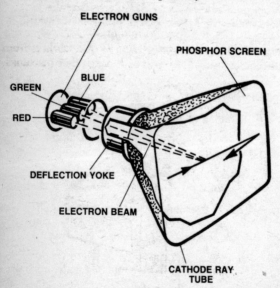

RGB monitor

ribbon cartridge The plastic holder and feed device for a printer ribbon. They vary considerably by type of printer.

ribbon cartridge

A RO <u>R</u>ead <u>O</u>nly (acronym). The ability to just read information from memory or storage and not to write to it.

robot A device capable of receiving input signals consisting of commands or information about environmental conditions and then using the information as a basis for performing mechanical, repetitive tasks. Robots are used primarily in industry to increase productivity, to free workers from mundane tasks, and to repair and make other machines.

robot

robotics A field of study that involves the use of robots to perform tasks in industrial and other environments.

rollover A keyboard encoding mechanism that eliminates error when more than one key is pressed at the same time.

B ROM Read Only Memory (acronym).

ROMable Code designed to be placed in ROM memory.

rotations In computer graphics, the turning of a computer-modeled object relative to an origin point in a coordinate system.

routine A set of coded instructions arranged in a proper sequence to direct the computer to perform a specific action. A program may contain many routines, although a routine itself may be considered a program.

A RPG Report Program Generation language (acronym). A high-level programming language popular for business applications.

C RPROM ReProgrammable Read Only Memory (acronym).

RS-232 or RS-232C A widely used electronic industry standard (EIA) connector for interfacing computers to peripheral devices. EIA standard RS-232C specifically defines a 25-pin connector and the data and control circuits and signals required to interface a terminal and a modem. The standard also is used in the intercommunication of other serial peripheral devices.

RS-232 connector

A RST <u>ReST</u>art (acronym).

A RTC <u>R</u>eal <u>T</u>ime <u>C</u>lock (acronym).

A R/W <u>R</u>ead/<u>W</u>rite (acronym).

save To record and store permanently a program or data on a storage device such as a floppy disk.

A SBC <u>S</u>ingle <u>B</u>oard <u>C</u>omputer (acronym).

schematic A drawing showing component interconnections of a circuit.

schematic symbols Stylized line drawings that represent various elements and are used universally.

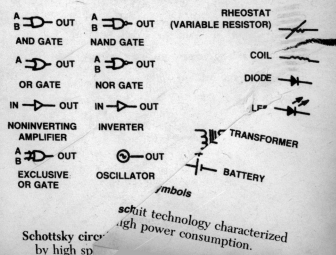

Schottsky circit technology characterized
by high sp...igh power consumption.

scientific notation A technique for expressing quantities as powers of ten; example, $12,300 = 1.23 \times 10^4$.

scratchpad An area of read/write memory used as a temporary work area.

screen dump The transfer of data or images from a terminal display to storage or to a peripheral device in order for it to be printed.

screen size The physical viewing dimension of a cathode ray tube (CRT) screen, usually expressed as a diagonal measure in inches. Screen size does not limit screen resolution.

screen type The technology of the display: cathode ray tube (CRT), liquid crystal display (LCD), light-emitting diode (LED), etc.

scrolling Moving text vertically or horizontally on a cathode ray tube (CRT) screen so that portions that do not fit on the screen at one time can be viewed. See horizontal scrolling; vertical scrolling.

search and replace The ability of a word processing program to find a specified character, word, or string each time it appears in the text and to replace it with another character, word, or string.

secondary storage Same as mass storage.

sectors An organization of data storage on a

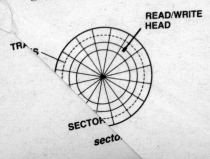

magnetic disk. Data are stored and accessed in a system of tracks and sectors.

seek time In a disk system, the time needed to move the read/write head to the required track position for a read.

segment A division of a program or a file in memory.

selection sort A sorting technique where one key (item of data) is designated as the lowest or highest. Then all of the remaining items in the list are compared and ordered in relation to that first key piece of data.

self-test The ability of a device, such as a printer, to run through all its operations and to test the internal circuitry to be sure it is working properly before proceeding with a specific task.

semiconductor A material that serves as an electronic conductor and has a resistance between that of a metal and an insulator. Its electrical conductivity is sensitive to the presence of impurities, and it varies with changes in the temperature around it. At high temperatures, it more closely resembles metal and has high conductivity, while at low temperatures it resists the electron flow. This property makes the element suitable for use as a transistor, functioning as a switch in a computer circuit.

sequential access See serial access.

serial access The process of obtaining data in a sequential fashion, so that in order to access an element all the preceding elements in that group must be searched through. Typically, this is the slowest of the access methods. Same as sequential access.

serial transmission The transmission of data in such a way that all the bits in a byte are handled one after another. Contrast with parallel transmission.

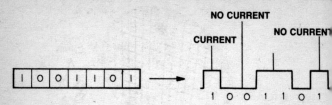

serial transmission

shift The operation of moving the binary contents of a storage register one or more bits to the left or right within the register in order to multiply or divide.

short-line seeking When a line to be printed does not span the entire page, the printer performs a carriage return at the end of the short line and begins to print a new line, speeding up printer performance.

B SIG Special Interest Group (acronym).

B SIGGRAPH Special Interest Group for GRAPHics (acronym). A nonprofit organization devoted to the advancement of computer graphics.

significant figures The number of digits in a number that are known to be entirely correct or to be meaningful for further use. For example, in computer calculations, numbers often are rounded off due to the restrictions of the word size. As these rounded-off numbers are used in additional calculations and are subsequently rounded off in turn, the numbers farthest to the right become less and less accurate. Therefore, although the computer may come up with a result that has 9 digits (as in 1.23456789) the last five digits may be unusable because they have become distorted by the calculation process itself. In this case, the number would be said to have "four significant figures"; i.e., 1.234.

silicon wafer A silicon ingot slice on which integrated

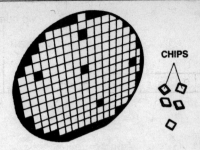

CHIPS

silicon wafer

circuits are fabricated. After fabrication and testing, the wafer is cut into individual chips, which are then used as finished integrated circuit components.

simplex A communications line that carries data from one point to another, in only one direction.

single-board computer A complete computer, including ROM, RAM, CPU, and I/O interface, implemented on a single printed circuit board. These frequently are used for industrial control applications.

single-purpose local-area network See network, local-area, single-purpose.

sixteen bit See microcomputer, 16-bit.

slave A device operating under the control of another device.

slave computer A computer used as a back-up when the primary computer fails. At any point in time the slave is mirroring the processing of the master computer.

slot A means of expanding microcomputer capabilities by adding circuit boards for specific applications. Slots are the receptacles that handle these boards.

slot bound A situation in which the expansion of a

microcomputer system becomes restricted by the number of expansion slots available to it.

smart peripheral A peripheral device, such as a terminal or printer, containing its own processor and memory so that it may relieve the host system of many functions normally associated with the functioning of that peripheral. Sometimes called an intelligent peripheral.

smart terminal A peripheral device that is used for data input and output and most often consists of a combined keyboard and CRT screen. A smart terminal has its own microprocessor and control electronics, allowing it to be useful "off-line" for certain functions. When it is "on-line," it may relieve the host processor and main memory of some duties associated with display. Contrast with dumb terminal.

smash Destruction of an area of memory or program by overwriting with another segment of memory or program.

B SNOBOL StriNg Oriented symBOlic Language (acronym). A high-level programming language geared toward manipulation of character strings.

soft error A transient, unpredictable fault usually associated with software rather than hardware.

soft keys Keys that can be defined in software for any nonprinting, nondisplay character functions such as erase, block move, etc. Also function keys.

soft sectors A floppy-disk formatting technique accomplished by software. The locations of sectors are determined by the distance of each sector from a photoelectrically sensed starting mark. Disks are searched by the operating system during initialization.

software Programs that tell the computer what operations to perform. Contrast with hardware.

soft-sectored disk

software package Ready-made programs offered by vendors or manufacturers to satisfy specific needs. Packages usually include the programs, stored on recording media, and documentation or tutorials.

software package

software, public domain See public-domain software.

solid state Electronic components, known for reliability and economy, that control electrons within solid materials (semiconductors). Their small size and suitability to mass production techniques have revolutionized electronic applications.

solid-state computer A computer built primarily from circuits and components containing semiconductors.

solids modeling Geometric modeling of an object by construction of a computer model based on the measurements, properties, and relationships of points, lines, angles, and surfaces of the object.

sort (1) To arrange data items according to identification criteria, such as identification (ID) number, alphabetical or numerical order, etc. (2) Rearrangement of input records to result in an ordered output file according to specified "keys," such as city, state, street, license number, etc.

Source, The™ An electronic information service operated by Source Telecomputing Corp., a subsidiary of the Reader's Digest Association, Inc. It is available to the public on a subscription basis and offers access to large data bases of varied information, electronic mail, shopping, software reviews, bulletin boards, etc.

source program The program in textual form, as input by the programmer.

space Binary 0, or no voltage.

Special-Interest Group (SIG). People who meet to discuss and exchange information about a specific computer-oriented interest, such as computer graphics, robotics, education, business applications, word processing, etc.

speech synthesizer A device that creates representations of speech from electronic phonemes using a set of rules that describe English pronunciations. It enables the computer to "talk" to its user.

spelling checker

spelling checker Software that proofreads by comparing each word in a text file to a dictionary, then marks and/or corrects misspelled words.

split screen A CRT screen display in which the software divides the screen into two or more separate sectional areas for independent viewing of portions of graphics, text, etc.

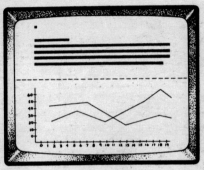

split screen

spooling Temporarily saving input/output data by means of a storage device for later use. For example, in word processing, the output can be spooled onto a floppy disk and then run off at the same time as the user is editing or otherwise using the microprocessor. See idle time.

spreadsheet, electronic See electronic spreadsheet.

sprocket feed See pin feed; tractor feed.

A SQ SQueeze (acronym). See squeezed files.

squeezed files (SQ). Normal data or program files that have been organized more efficiently using squeeze (SQ) and unsqueeze (USQ) utilities to save space and reduce transfer time.

stack A block of successive memory locations organized on a last-in-first-out (LIFO) basis to preserve the ordering of information that is necessary to certain functions. See LIFO.

stack pointer See pointer.

stair stepping Refers to the discontinuous nature of
a line drawn by a raster display at any angle other
than vertical, horizontal, or 45 degrees. The raster
display must approximate the line because of the
limitations of its technology and resolution.

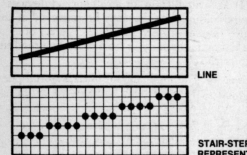

LINE

STAIR-STEPPED
REPRESENTATION

stair stepping

start bit A bit whose only function is to indicate the
start of a character (1 byte) in an asynchronous
transmission of data. See asynchronous communication.

STAT Status (abbreviation).

state-of-the-art The most current research and
up-to-date technology in a specific field of
knowledge.

static RAM A type of memory storage, it will retain
its contents indefinitely without refreshing
(regeneration) so long as power is supplied. Contrast
with dynamic RAM.

static turtle In the Logo language, a turtle (cursor)
with a fixed spatial position and heading that
responds to such commands as FORWARD and
LEFT. See turtle graphics.

status (STAT). The condition of a device at a specified
time.

stepper motor An electromechanical device that

moves or rotates by a fixed amount each time an electrical pulse is applied to it. Often found in printers, disk drives, and other computer equipment.

stop bit A bit that comes at the end of each character in an asynchronous serial transmission.

storage (1) An overall term for a category of devices capable of holding data that may be retrieved at any time once they have been input. (2) The act of putting data into memory or on a recording medium for later retrieval.

storage capacity The total amount of data stored per unit of media and which may be accessed by the system without changing media.

storage media Refers to the type of medium used; disk, cassette tape, hard disk, mag cards, etc.

storage tube A display technology that behaves like a cathode ray tube (CRT) screen, but which has extremely long-persistence phosphors that retain their charge for hours. The picture will remain on the screen for hours rather than for the fraction of a second common to dynamic storage, eliminating the need for refresh or frame buffers. Storage tubes excel in high resolution unmatched by raster systems, although they are not as well suited as raster systems for color graphics or interactive applications.

store To place data or programs in the computer for later use.

streaming A technique for rapid recording on a magnetic tape, usually for backing up a Winchester disk system. Streaming eliminates the gaps and short-stops between data blocks often produced by other recording methods, thereby speeding data transfer.

string An organized and connected set of characters. Example: the word "data" is a string of 4 characters.

string length The number of characters in a string.

strobe A hardware control signal for information transfer.

structured language A computer language that fosters structured programming techniques through its use of vocabulary, syntax, and grammar. See structured programming.

structured programming A programming methodology developed to simplify the design, debugging, testing, and documentation functions associated with computer programming. Structured language is best known for its use of modules and its attempt to reduce drastically or eliminate the GOTO branches in computer programming.

B STRUDL STRuctural Design Language (acronym). A language used for design and analysis of structures.

stylus A penlike device used with a graphics tablet for inputting position information relative to a coordinate axes system employed by the tablet.

stylus

B SUB SUBroutine (acronym).

subprogram Program segments that perform a specific function. They are stored in a library and are combined as part of a larger program when needed. If the function is used in many programs, a subprogram offers reduced programming and debugging labor. In contrast to subroutines, which usually are available only to one program, subprograms are available for use by many programs.

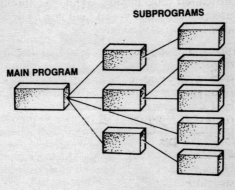

subprogram

subroutine (SUB). A program module outside the main program that can be called repeatedly by the main program. It can perform any mathematical or logical routine of which the main routine is capable. Control is transferred from the main program to the subroutine and is returned after the subroutine carries out its function. Contrast with subprogram.

subroutine

subscript Characters printed below the normal line of type as in $_{sub}$script; for example, $A_1 + B_2$.

superscript Characters printed above the normal line of type as in ^{super}script; for example, $x^2 + y^4$.

support In computer practice, the promise by vendors of help and guidance in using purchased or leased software and hardware.

surge A sudden voltage or current change in an electrical circuit. It can cause a microcomputer and its peripherals to give erroneous results or to stop functioning.

surge protector A device that plugs into the wall socket to protect microcomputers from alternating current (AC) line surges. The computer plugs into the surge protector. See surge.

surge protector

symbolic language A set of instructions to the computer that is understandable by humans because of the Englishlike nature of the language. A symbolic language still must be translated to machine language for execution.

synchronization Coordination of signals to ensure that receiver and transmitter are operating in phase with one another.

synchronous data communication A transmission of data in which transmitting and receiving devices are synchronized to a common clock signal. Contrast with asynchronous transmission.

syntax The set of grammatical rules defining the structure of a programming language.

B SYSGEN SYStem GENeration (acronym). A process for initializing and generating an operating system in a computer.

systems analyst A person who examines and defines activities, work flow, and problems to be solved, as well as systems and procedures, in order to determine how the necessary operations can best be accomplished. The situation usually is reviewed in terms of a computer environment.

systems software Programs that control the execution of user or applications programs and that include compilers, assemblers, debuggers, utilities, and operating systems. These are usually supplied by the hardware manufacturer.

tabbing Sending a printer head or display cursor to a preset column position on the paper or screen.

table look-up The process of searching through an array of data (a table) using logic in a computer routine to find a specific value.

tag A unit of information with a composition that differs from that of other members of the set so that it can be used as a marker or label. This unit is given a name or a memory location to make it easier to reference.

tape cartridge Magnetic tape in a cartridge used with a tape drive, usually for the purpose of media back-up for a disk. The data cartridges can be high capacity, holding as much as 20 megabytes of unformatted data, and data can be transferred quickly in a streaming mode.

tape, cassette See audio cassette tape.

tape, magnetic See magnetic tape.

tape reel A magnetic tape wound around a spool and referred to collectively as a tape reel. These units are generally used with industry standard magnetic tape storage systems.

tape reel

telecommunications The transmission of information via phone lines, cables, optical fibers, TV, FM radio waves, satellite transmission, etc.

teleprinter Any device employing a keyboard integrated with a printer and used for telecommunications.

Teletype™ Trademark of the Teletype Corp. One of the first peripheral devices used for sending and

Teletype ™ machine

receiving messages with a computer. A teletype is characterized by high reliability, noisy operation, and low cost. It also has relatively slow printing speeds of about 10 characters per second and slow transmission rates of 110 baud.

Telex™ An international network of teleprinter subscribers.

text editor A program or set of routines in a computer system, most often used by programmers to edit a source program. It allows the user to enter, change, order, output, or delete information.

thermal printer A small-format, nonimpact printer that forms characters by applying heat to special heat-sensitive papers. Thermal printers have slow speeds, mediocre quality reproduction, and expensive paper overhead. However, they have low initial cost and are able to combine easily graphic and alphanumerical output.

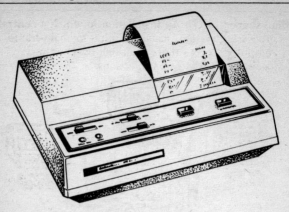

thermal printer

thimble print element A plastic thimble-shaped element containing flat spokes with raised characters. The thimble rotates, positioning the spokes so that the striking device can hit the spoke tip against the ribbon; this action imprints the character onto the paper.

thimble print element

third-party lease An arrangement in which an independent firm buys equipment from the manufacturer and in turn leases it to the end user. The middle-man firm is called the "third party."

three-dimensional digitizer See digitizer, three-dimensional.

time sharing (T/S). An installation in which a central processing system, usually a mini- or main-frame computer, serves more than one user, either locally or by telecommunications.

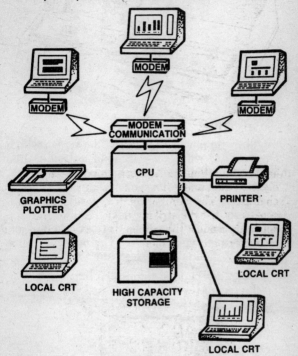

time sharing

token May be used to refer to the code word for a macroinstruction.

top-of-forms set A forms-handling ability that can advance paper automatically to a preset position and that is initiated by receipt of a form-feed character. This can be accomplished by hardware or software.

touch terminal A terminal with which the user

touch terminal

physically interacts by touching the screen with a finger in order to choose an input instead of using traditional input devices such as keyboards, digitizers, or light pens.

A **tpi** tracks per inch (acronym).

trace A listing of all the steps that had taken place during a software procedure. The purpose is to help locate sources of logic error.

trackball A device used to position the cursor on the screen by various rotations of the

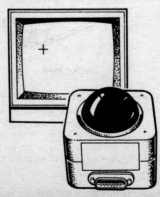

trackball

ball mechanism. Once the intended cursor position is reached, the device can send a signal which sends the cursor coordinates to the system.

tracks A physical organization in the form of concentric rings, used to store data on a magnetic disk. The arrangement is similar to that of a phonograph record. However, any location on a track can be accessed directly, without a sequential search. Each track is divided into sectors. See sectors.

tracks per inch (tpi). A unit of measurement for track density on a floppy disk.

tractor feed A printer attachment that guides paper using advancing sprockets, or pins, that fit into holes in the paper. The method yields more precise alignment than friction feed methods. Same as pin feed.

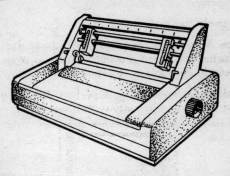

tractor feed

transaction listing (1) A record of everything that has happened on a system. Same as system log. (2) A listing of all transactions processed in a user program. Same as audit trail.

transceiver A device or circuit capable of both receiving and transmitting.

transient Fast, temporary variations in a line voltage.

transistor An electronic device that uses semiconductor properties to control the flow of current.

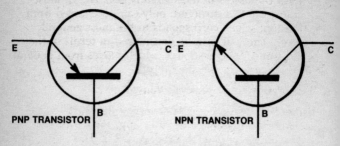

transistor, schematic representation

translation In computer graphics, the displacement of a computer-modeled object when it is moved from one position to another along a set of coordinate axes.

translator A program that converts a sequence of statements in one language into corresponding statements in another language. Interpreters, assemblers, and compilers are types of translators.

transmission speed The speed at which data are transmitted over a communications line, expressed in bits per second (bps). For most consumer needs, the bit rate is roughly equal to the baud rate.

transparent Changes or operations in the computer program or system are said to be transparent when they are not noticeable by the user but are necessary to carry out instruction commands or functions. For example, a change that speeds up a processing function but does not change a user's interaction with the program would be transparent. The term can pertain to hardware or software changes.

tree structure A hierarchical method of indicating data relationships, a tree structure promotes efficient search and retrieval of data. In "traveling down the logic tree," the user makes a series of binary choices that exclude unwanted possibilities until the object of the search is isolated. In most cases, the tree structure only can be entered from the top, which corresponds to the most general level. The logic can be considered in terms of the old game "20 Questions," which moves from general to increasingly specific queries.

A TRS Tandy Radio Shack (acronym).

truncation The process of dropping the least significant digits of a number (e.g., in 2.9783, dropping the .0083 to produce 2.97). The resulting loss of precision is usually in favor of greater speed or simplified handling due to a reduction in storage requirements. Since only a certain number of digits can be fit into a computer word, the amount of truncation required depends on the machine's word size. The larger the word size, the less truncation is required and the greater the accuracy. See word size.

truth table A mathematical table that states input values and lists all possible combinations (Boolean relationships) of output values as a function of the input. See Boolean Algebra; AND; OR; NOR.

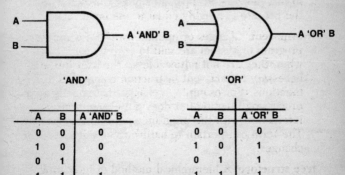

A	B	A 'AND' B
0	0	0
1	0	0
0	1	0
1	1	1

A	B	A 'OR' B
0	0	0
1	0	1
0	1	1
1	1	1

truth tables

A T/S _Time _Sharing (acronym).

A TSS _Time _Sharing _System (acronym).

T switch A device that allows two peripherals to share a common third component or input/output port.

A TTY _Tele_TYpewriter (acronym). Also teletype machine.

turnaround time A measure of system performance based on the elapsed time from the submission of a job until the receipt of some form of output.

turnkey A system or installation that is complete and ready to run without further additions or modifications.

turtle The name for a small triangular pointer on a display screen, which is used with the Logo language to implement turtle graphics. See turtle graphics.

turtle geometry A new mathematics based on turtle movements in the Logo language.

turtle graphics Drawings created on a computer display or output device using the Logo educational program. Commands are sent to a turtle (cursor). Following the specific Logo commands, the turtle can move around the screen and draw

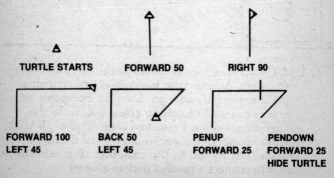

| TURTLE STARTS | FORWARD 50 | RIGHT 90 |

| FORWARD 100 LEFT 45 | BACK 50 LEFT 45 | PENUP FORWARD 25 | PENDOWN FORWARD 25 HIDE TURTLE |

turtle graphics

lines. Concepts of programming and coordinate systems can be taught to children (and adults) using this approach.

tutorial (1) Lessons, classes, demonstrations covering a subject area. (2) Instructions about running hardware and/or software, usually in manual or program form.

type ball A molded metal printer element shaped like a golf ball, with raised characters set around the surface. It is mounted on a movable axis and acts as a hammer, striking the ribbon against the paper to produce the character image.

type ball

U

C UART Universal Asynchronous Receiver/Transmitter (acronym). A large-scale integration logic circuit that converts parallel input from the computer into asynchronous serial data for transmission. In the other direction (for a received transmission), UART translates received asynchronous serial data into parallel bits for use by the computer. It is normally used to connect a parallel port to a serial communication network.

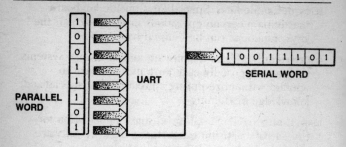

UART

A UCSD Pascal Un̲iversity of C̲alifornia, S̲an D̲iego Pascal (acronym). A version of the Pascal language developed at that University.

UCSD p-System An operating system for small computers developed at the University of California, San Diego.

A UG U̲ser G̲roup (acronym).

A UHF U̲ltra H̲igh F̲requencies (acronym).

ultraviolet erasing Use of a high-intensity shortwave ultraviolet light to erase the contents of an EPROM chip. See EPROM.

unconditional branch An instruction used to transfer control to another part of the program regardless of the results of previous instructions.

UNIX™ An operating system developed by Bell Laboratories for minicomputers, which is now being rewritten for microcomputer systems.

C USART U̲niversal S̲ynchronous/A̲synchronous R̲eceiver/T̲ransmitter (acronym). A peripheral device that converts parallel data from the central processing unit (CPU) into a serial stream of data for transmission. At the same time, it can receive and convert serial data into parallel bits for use by the computer. USART differs from UART and USRT in that it can communicate by means of both synchronous and asynchronous techniques.

user-definable keys Special keys on the keyboard that initiate certain operations in the program; the keys, functions can be defined by the user.

user friendly Refers to software and hardware systems that are supposedly easy for a user to learn to operate without requiring a great deal of specialized knowledge or training.

user group (UG). People who share information for the use of a specific computer system, or software, through meetings and/or publications.

user hotline Direct telephone access to a manufacturer, who provides end users with answers to technical questions concerning their products.

user interaction Active communication between the computer system and the user. A user entry will cause a direct response by the system. Also called interactive systems.

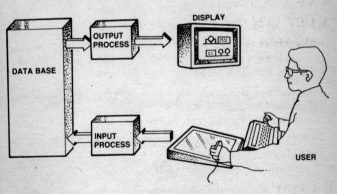

user interaction

user memory Central processing unit (CPU) memory that can be accessed and changed by the user. It usually refers to the portion of random access memory that is used by application programs.

C USRT <u>U</u>niversal <u>S</u>ynchronous <u>R</u>eceiver/<u>T</u>ransmitter (acronym). A high-speed transmission converter that differs from UART in that it is a synchronous device. When the computer sends a message through USRT for transmission, the parallel bits are converted to a serial stream. When receiving serial bits, USRT converts the serial data into parallel words. Because it is a synchronous device, USRT depends on a timing system rather than on the start and stop bits used in UART. See UART.

utility functions Functions that are used to perform common system procedures such as printing, moving data, reading from disk, etc.

utility routines A group of system programs, usually supplied by the hardware or operating system vendor. Their purpose is to carry out specific, vital functions necessary to the operation of a computer system. These "housekeeping" functions keep the system running smoothly and include (but are not limited to) copying programs, reordering programs, listings of operations, etc.

variable A symbol used in a program to represent a quantity with a value that can be reassigned during the course of program execution.

variable length record file A file that contains records of varying length. Contrast with "fixed-length record file."

vectored interrupt A technique in which each interrupting device provides an address at the time of the interrupt request, enabling the operating system to branch to the appropriate interrupt routine. This results in increased efficiency in determining which device is requesting attention, as compared to use of a polling technique.

vertical scrolling Ability of the system to move up and down through a page or more of data that are displayed on the terminal screen.

vertical scrolling

very large scale integration (VLSI). The process of fabricating integrated circuits on a silicon chip that contains up to 100,000 semiconductor devices.

video bandwidth The number of dots per second that can be displayed on a television screen or computer monitor. The greater the bandwidth, the higher the number of characters that can be displayed clearly at one time.

video computer A computer designed principally for running commercially produced cartridges that contain games and rote learning programs.

video computer

video-disk system A mass storage technology that uses optical lasers to record information by burning holes in a tellurium medium. One disk can hold about 55,000 pages of information.

video-disk system

video monitor A display unit that resembles a television set but does not have a speaker or apparatus for detecting UHF/VHF frequencies. A monitor does have a direct video connection and

accepts higher bandwidth than a television,
allowing more characters to be displayed clearly at
one time. Since the monitor has no local
intelligence or control electronics, the computer
must contain appropriate interfaces to control the
monitor.

video monitor

video signal Refers to an electronic signal that
conveys all necessary information (color, intensity,
location, synchronization) about each position on
the screen so that the image is placed properly on
the screen.

virtual address An address or memory location in a
virtual memory system; i.e., the location of the
address is unrelated to the actual physical location
where the data reside in memory. The logical
address will be translated into a physical address by
the operating system so that it can be used by the
program. See virtual memory. Contrast with
absolute address.

virtual memory A system that allows the processor to
address memory space beyond the limits of
physical memory. In a microcomputer, this is
achieved by operating system software that places
portions of the user's software and data in auxiliary
storage. When the data are required for
execution, the system swaps currently unused
material in main memory for the needed sections
residing in auxiliary storage and adjusts addresses as

needed. With a virtual memory system, the storage capacity appears to be much larger than its actual size.

VisiCalc™ This was the first electronic spreadsheet software written for the personal computer. It enables solution of mathematical problems through use of a grid system set up on the video screen.

A **VLSI** Very Large Scale Integration (acronym).

C **VMOS** V-channel Metal Oxide Semiconductor (acronym). A type of NMOS technology in which a V-shaped notch is used to improve density. Sometimes used for high-density dynamic RAM chips.

voice recognition A system that accepts a vocabulary of clearly spoken words as input commands.

volatile memory Memory that does not retain its information content when the power is turned off.

von Neumann, John Usually credited with formulating the concept of a stored program computer; i.e., controlling the computer by means of a program stored in the computer's internal memory.

C **VTOC** Volume Table Of Contents (acronym). A catalog used by the operating system to locate data or program files; the files usually reside on disk.

W

W Write (acronym).

wafer See silicon wafer.

wait state The state of the microprocessor unit when it is not being used to process data. See idle time.

Wangnet™ A local area network (LAN) system offered by Wang Laboratories, Inc. See network, local-area.

Winchester disk A type of hard-disk drive system initially developed by IBM, it has a sealed nonremovable rigid magnetic oxide-coated disk. It offers very short access time and high-capacity storage as compared with cassette tapes or floppy-disk drives.

Winchester disk system

window An isolated portion of a cathode ray tube screen that is used to display information independently of the rest of the screen display.

wire-frame representation A three-dimensional representation of an object with hidden lines shown, giving the impression of a transparent object with only its structure visible. See hidden line.

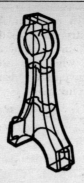

wire-frame representation

word processing The implementation of word
processor software on a computer for writing,
editing, revising, manipulating, formatting, and
printing text for letters, reports, and manuscripts.

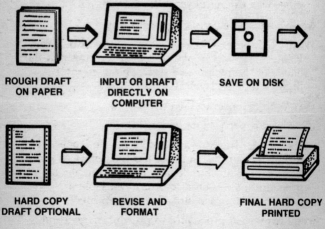

ROUGH DRAFT ON PAPER   **INPUT OR DRAFT DIRECTLY ON COMPUTER**   **SAVE ON DISK**

HARD COPY DRAFT OPTIONAL   **REVISE AND FORMAT**   **FINAL HARD COPY PRINTED**

word processing

word size A fixed number of bits, dependent on the
hardware architecture, and which serves as the
basic logical unit of information. The central
processing unit processes and transfers each word
as a separate entity. In microprocessors, word sizes

are commonly 8, 16, or 32 bit. A larger word size requires fewer instructions per data move. One instruction on a 16-bit machine may move 2 characters of data, while one instruction on an 8-bit machine would move only 1 character. See microcomputer architecture.

| 7 | 6 | 5 | 4 | 3 | 2 | 1 | 0 | BINARY DIGIT NUMBER |

BINARY DIGITS

8-BIT WORD

| 15 | 14 | 13 | 12 | 11 | 10 | 9 | 8 | 7 | 6 | 5 | 4 | 3 | 2 | 1 | 0 |

16-BIT WORD

word size

word wrap In word processing automatic placement of a word on the next line if that word would otherwise extend beyond the margin.

worksheet See electronic spreadsheet.

World Computer Citizen A center located in Paris, France, devoted to placing computer power in the hands of the people and expanding computer literacy to benefit every world citizen.

WP Word Processing (acronym).

wpm words per minute (acronym).

write-enable To allow access to a device, such as a disk drive, so that the user has the ability to put information into the device. A write-enable procedure is required in order to disable a write-protect procedure. See write-protect.

write-protect A procedure to prevent inadvertent writing over of previously stored information on a storage medium, such as a disk. With a floppy disk, a protective tab may be placed on the write-protect notch of the jacket to control this feature. With a hard-disk drive, a switch would be engaged; with a tape, a plastic ring first must be removed from the tape.

C XOR e<u>X</u>clusive <u>OR</u> (acronym).

A z <u>z</u>ero bit (acronym).

zap (1) Intentional use of a command found in many programs to clear the screen. (2) To unintentionally overwrite a file.

ZILOG Manufacturers of microprocessors, including the Z-80 and the Z-80A.

Z-Net A local area network (LAN) system similar to Ethernet™. See network, local-area.

BANTAM IS PLUGGED IN TO COMPUTERS

MONEY TALKS!
How to get it and How to keep it!

☐	23489	SALARY STRATEGIES by Marilyn Moats Kennedy	$3.50
☐	05025	ALL YOU NEED TO KNOW ABOUT BANKS by John Cook & Robert Wool (Hardcover)	$13.95
☐	23568	GET A JOB IN 60 SECONDS by Steve Kravette	$2.95
☐	22850	MONEYWISE by Mimi Brien	$3.50
☐	22509	THE BOOK OF FIVE RINGS by Miyamoto Musashi	$2.95
☐	22936	HOW TO GET FREE TAX HELP by Matthew Lesko	$2.95
☐	23455	YOU CAN NEGOTIATE ANYTHING by Herb Cohen	$3.95
☐	23160	GUERRILLA TACTICS IN THE JOB MARKET by T. Jackson	$3.50
☐	23563	THE ONLY INVESTMENT GUIDE YOU'LL EVER NEED by Andrew Tobias	$3.95
☐	23453	HOW TO WAKE UP THE FINANCIAL GENIUS INSIDE YOU by Mark Oliver Haroldsen	$3.50
☐	20296	THE COMING CURRENCY COLLAPSE: And What You Can Do About It.	$3.95
☐	20478	THE COMPLETE BOOK OF HOME BUYING by M. Sumichrast & R. Shafer	$3.95
☐	23099	THE GAMESMAN: The New Corporate Leaders by Michael Maccoby	$3.95
☐	22909	THE GREATEST SALESMAN IN THE WORLD by Og Mandino	$2.75
☐	22550	ALMOST EVERYONE'S GUIDE TO ECONOMICS by Galbraith/Salinge	$2.95
☐	20191	HIGH FINANCE ON A LOW BUDGET by Mark Skousen	$2.95

Prices and availability subject to change without notice.

Buy them at your local bookstore or use this handy coupon for ordering:

We Deliver!
And So Do These Bestsellers.

PAID